The
VISION KEEPERS

Walkers sitting in a circle in Washington, D.C.

The VISION KEEPERS

WALKING *for*
NATIVE AMERICANS *and*
the EARTH

DOUG ALDERSON

Quest Books
Theosophical Publishing House

Wheaton, Illinois ◆ Chennai (Madras), India

Copyright © 2007 by Doug Alderson

First Quest edition 2007

Quest Books
The Theosophical Publishing House
P.O. Box 270
Wheaton, IL 60189-0270

www.questbooks.net

Cover image: © Joel Nakamura/Images.com
Cover design, book design, and typesetting by Dan Doolin

Library of Congress Cataloging-in-Publication Data
Alderson, Doug.
The vision keepers: walking for Native Americans and the Earth /
Doug Alderson. — 1st Quest Books ed.
p.   cm.
Includes bibliographical references and index.
ISBN-13: 978-0-8356-0851-0
ISBN-10: 0-8356-0851-4
1. Indians of North America—Social life and customs.   2. Indian philosophy—North America.   3. Indigenous peoples—Ecology—North America.   I. Title.
E98.S7A43 2007
305.897—dc22   2006034434

Printed in the United States of America

5   4   3   2   1   *   07   08   09   10   11

To all the walkers

In beauty all day long, may I walk.

Through the returning seasons, may I walk.

On the trail marked with pollen, may I walk.

With dew about my feet, may I walk.

With beauty before me, may I walk.

With beauty behind me, may I walk.

With beauty below me, may I walk.

With beauty above me, may I walk.

With beauty all around me, may I walk.

—Traditional Navajo Prayer Song

CONTENTS

PREFACE

A friend suggested that the section of this book describing a walk across the United States in which I participated be entitled A Walk through Reagan's America. "It took place during the eighties, the era of the Cold War, and the eighties are 'in' now," he said. "That title will sell."

I smiled politely. He was trying to be helpful, but I explained that the walks I recount in this book had very little to do with Cold War politics. Collectively, they are a journey through Native America and across the earth.

One major theme runs throughout the entire human experience: the spiritual quest. It is about seeking, receiving, and following a vision. Challenges and roadblocks seem a necessary part of this quest, in that they serve to strengthen, resolve, and clarify values.

Many young people—and those of all ages—seem lost because they haven't found their vision. They haven't taken the time and effort required for sincere introspection, and they haven't received the proper guidance and support from their elders and spiritual leaders. Visions aren't found in video games, television sets, or computers. In my opinion, spending quiet time in nature affords the best opportunity. Initially, a journey on the Appalachian Trail worked for me; others can find their own way.

Fortunately, following my initial spiritual awakening I met a gifted teacher, Bear Heart, who guided me through the next step. A teacher often comes forth when he or she is needed most, although not always in the form you might expect.

Early in my relationship with Bear Heart, I asked for his permission to write about my experiences. He encouraged me to do so, understanding that writing was part of my purpose. I have tried to be tactful by not using full names or the real names of certain persons. My purpose has been not to identify anyone who might receive unwelcome attention. If I have unwittingly done so, I apologize. Overall, I have sought to write the truth as I perceive it about experiences meant to be shared. Some of them may seem far-fetched, especially during my time with Bear Heart, but I have striven to record them exactly as they occurred. All I ask is that you view them with an open mind.

While some of the elders and spiritual teachers I describe have "gone home," meaning that their physical bodies have ceased to exist, it is my hope that their messages and examples will live on in these pages. They continue to guide from other realms.

For me, writing this book has been like giving birth. The impact of certain profound experiences had been gestating for a long time, and, when it was time for the book to emerge, the process was both joyful and challenging. Now, with a sense of satisfaction and some trepidation, I present this "child" to the world.

ACKNOWLEDGMENTS

This book would not have been possible without the many people who helped to organize and participate in the walks described herein. They shared in my visions and offered many of their own. In alphabetical order, some of those folks include Steve Alderson, Theo Bailey, Meret (Claudia) Bainbridge, Sandra Bell, Mindi Bender, Matthew Bennett, Ursula (Wilhoit) Boutmy, Robert Glenn Breckenridge, Hal Brill, Sharon (Sierra) Bruckner, Irineo Cabreros, Suzanne (Schmidt) Carlson, Marie Cavaroc, Ralph Cobb, Tom Cockrell, Elladon Dagsson, Ann Davenport, Chip Davenport, Will Fudeman, Ron Greenlight Griffith, Dabney Hammer, Eric Herminghausen, Barbara Hirshkowitz, Kim Hubbell, Cyndi Hunt, Jon Jon Jackson, Priscilla Johnson, Eddy Long, Jerry Lunsford, Al Maher, Eric Stoller Mann, Maria Marcussen, Alice Massie, John Montrose, One Eagle Morrow, Leslie (Goodwoman) Nathanson, Dave Norberg, Avraham (Coyote) Novick, Sarah (Allison) Novick, April Perdue, Michael Perdue, Leslie and Psalm Pollock, Indigo Andrea Raffel, A. J. Richardson, Robin Rieske, Dale Robinson, Julie Rogers, Water Sadauskas, Joe Schetter, Mark Seckman, Mikel Schoelen, Anthony Silva, Susie Stahl, Katherine Stanley, Lee Lee Ammidon Sutton, Ruth Tonachel, Calvin Trampleasure, Stuart Tregoning, Victoria Tregoning, Debbie Tyson, Eric White, Rosie White, and Johannes Vorholzer. They came from all across the country and other lands, from all walks of life, and I am proud to call them my friends. Thank you.

I also want to express appreciation to my family for their support: my wife, Cyndi, and daughter, Cheyenne; my parents, John and Jeanne; my brothers and their spouses, Dave and Sarah and Steve and Hua; and Alexia, Gareth, and Joey. I also want to thank the Barnum, Olmstead, and Rudow families. You have been great to me over the years, in all of my pursuits.

Many people think a book is finished when you've penned the last page. That is only stage one. I want to express appreciation to the good folks at Quest Books, especially to Richard Smoley for his guidance early on and to Sharron Dorr for her thorough job of editing. Sharron posed insightful questions and suggestions that prompted a great deal of head scratching and intense research on my part. Her input helped to round out the book.

Part
ONE

THE CALL OF A VISION

Chapter
1

THE TORCH IS PASSED

D read was setting in. I was nearing the halfway point on the Appalachian Trail, and my hiking companions had returned home for a break. I myself was anticipating a short "vacation" from the trail. My parents would meet me in Duncannon, Pennsylvania, in three days, but I would have to hike the forty-odd miles to town alone. Three days of solitude for an eighteen year old—that was an eternity.

Already, I had suffered through numerous blisters while hiking over steep and rugged mountains in Maine and New Hampshire. Several streams and a wide, rock-bottomed river—the Kennebec—required fording. Consecutive days of rain, along with incessant clouds of black flies, mosquitoes, and no-see-ums, challenged my will to proceed. Through it all, I had been with trail friends, sharing the challenges, joys, and miseries of trail life. Now, I was alone, and the solitude left me feeling quiet and subdued. Memories of a lost love—my most serious high school romance—came flooding back to me. Almost a thousand miles of walking had not seemed to ease my anguish.

I tried to shift my thinking. There was no one with whom to share the pain, no sympathetic ears or nods of understanding, and so I began talking to rocks and trees, valleys and mountaintops, insects and hawks. These things, to me, represented the Creator. I bared my soul without inhibition. And slowly, quietly, it seemed that something, some form of consciousness, was listening.

The earth answered in a way that a river does when it flows shallowly over rocks, or the wind does when it bends the hemlocks. My pangs of isolation gradually disappeared. A pure sensation came over me, a feeling of oneness. My footsteps slowed. I breathed in deep and full, often pausing to gaze upon valleys below and at trees and streams and soaring raptors. I was filling up, soaking up life. Soon, I saw more than the land before me; I could feel it, really feel it, as if the reach of my consciousness had become miles wide and miles deep.

After more hours of hiking, I began to see a strong image in my mind's eye—a vision—of a man about thirty years of age speaking before a large gathering of people, with blue mountains in the background. I sensed a strong spiritual unity and a Native American presence centered on an ecological purpose. I knew what this man was saying and even mouthed some of his words. More importantly, I felt the power of his message: Protect the environment and unite with our traditional Native American brothers and sisters.

The man, I soon realized, was I myself at a future date. My purpose? To speak on behalf of Mother Earth.

The vision stayed with me for the remainder of my long journey to Georgia. Now I understood my purpose, but how would it manifest?

A few months after returning to Tallahassee, having completed the trail on a snowy November morning at Springer Mountain, I sought to regain the peace of the Appalachian Mountains by revisiting a place of my boyhood. It was a scenic pond—Stewart's Pond—a few blocks from my home and less than two miles from Florida's capitol building. A nursery had once operated on the west bank; with the nursery's closure, the area had returned to its wild state, covered only with tall pines, sabal palm, moss-draped maple, sweetgum, water oak, and fragrant willow and wax myrtle. The greenery and sweet aromas enfolded me as if in a pleasant embrace.

Stewart's Pond would be my Walden, I thought, a haven of sanity close to home. Such places can be guideposts in one's life, like age-old landmarks of the walkabout. People around you change. You change. But some places don't seem to change. When you return to them, you can see how far you've come since your last visit; you can glimpse a future direction.

Leaving the pond's lush banks that day, small black-and-white signs greeted me: Lot 1, Lot 2, Lot 3. . . . A housing development would soon encircle the pond if action were not taken. Not hesitating, that very night I launched a campaign. Letters urging that Stewart's Pond be saved were soon on their way to park officials, city commissioners, the newspaper editor, and environmental groups. I stuffed flyers into mailboxes and newspapers of people living in the area. I wrote or called anyone who might assist. I even contacted the pond's owners, begging them to donate all or part of the area for a park, but with no success. Soon, however, my phone started ringing from people wanting to help. Television stations and other media became interested. The effort to protect Stewart's Pond was underway.

The movement grew to where the issue was scheduled to come up before the Tallahassee City Commission. Commissioners would consider purchasing the pond and its immediate environs—twenty acres in all—as a nature park. Nervously, I readied myself for the meeting. I had done very little public speaking and none outside of school. My palms started sweating at the mere thought.

Just before the evening meeting, I flipped on the local news and watched, horrified, as footage showed a yellow bulldozer clearing the first lot along Stewart's Pond. The machine's shiny blade sliced into my heart. Time was running out, or maybe it was already too late? Chagrined, my father and I drove to the city council meeting. We took our seats on uncomfortable metal chairs while commissioners read through minutes of the last meeting and took up other issues. Only a handful of pond supporters were in attendance, people who lived within a block of the pond. Not exactly a groundswell of support.

When the commission chairman finally reached the agenda item, I was a wreck. I nervously stumbled to the podium, hands shaking, and was able only to blurt out my name, address, and a brief statement asking the city to purchase the pond and protect it as a natural oasis within the city limits. That was it. The bulk of my planned speech remained on paper.

Commissioners began to debate the item. Most agreed that the purchase price was too high—$400,000—four times the appraised value. Moreover, there were already other parks in the area, one being an algae-covered pond a mile away, where people contributed to the obesity of hybrid ducks by giving them generous helpings of stale bread.

The proposal was about to die when a soft-spoken woman, a few years older than I, stood up. "I'd like to speak on this issue," she said. The mayor gave her five minutes. Glenda was her name. In a most eloquent, heart-filled voice, she spoke of growing up near the pond, of witnessing the destruction and development of many local green spaces, and of her sincere desire to protect this one place where she could bring her nieces and nephews to see natural Florida. Her words seemed to reach into my being and express everything I felt about the earth, about the importance of being close to nature, and about the need to preserve places like Stewart's Pond for future generations.

I began to weep, loudly, right there in the meeting, unable to stop. My vision on the Appalachian Trail had filled me with purpose, but expressing or fulfilling that purpose was a different matter. The last time I had wept in public was at age seven when Bambi's mother died on the movie screen. I leaned against my father, thankful he didn't shrink away in embarrassment, while Glenda gave voice to the natural world. Her speech caused more serious deliberation among the commissioners; one of them, a large man named Ben Thompson, advocated for the pond's purchase. Lifting my tear-stained face, I felt a glimmer of hope.

In the end, however, the cause was lost. Stewart's Pond was just another oasis lost to the oncoming tide of "progress." Through my tears, I vowed to become a better spokesperson for Mother Earth and not to let anxiety prevent me from speaking my heart. Maybe other Waldens were in need of rescuing.

A week after the hearing, I was hiking with a Florida Trail Association group through the Apalachicola National Forest and met Betty Watts, an intrepid gray-haired outdoorswoman and author. She had seen a small blurb about Stewart's Pond in the local newspaper. Being active in a Sierra Club group, she urged me to continue my activism. She later invited me to dinner at her house. After serving generous helpings of scrumptious baked chicken, fixings, and apple pie, Betty began her pitch.

"I'm getting on in years and becoming more forgetful these days," she began sadly. "I need someone to take over my duties as wilderness chair for the club. Could you do it?"

"Me?" I blubbered. "I have no idea what to do."

"Don't worry," she assured me, "You have what it takes right here." She touched my heart with a wrinkled hand. "Everything else will follow." It was an archetypal moment—the elder passing the torch to a younger protégé.

Despite my trepidation, I agreed. Betty promptly produced a detailed list of tasks requiring immediate attention. Within days, I was meeting with state officials about state park issues and with federal officials about issues concerning Florida's three national forests. I also began spearheading a drive to halt intensive timber operations on a nearby wildlife refuge. Part of the vision I had had on the Appalachian Trail was being fulfilled, but only part. What of the Native American presence I had sensed? How could I connect with indigenous people in a land where there didn't seem to be any? While working on behalf of the environment, I waited patiently for an opportunity.

Chapter

2

BEAR HEART

He didn't quite fulfill the image I had of a full-blooded Native American. He wore pointed cowboy boots, jeans, and a button-down shirt. Only a few feathers protruded from the side of his cowboy hat—small ones of the red flicker. His black hair was cropped short, and, when he smiled, it was apparent he was missing bottom teeth. His face was roundish, his skin dark, his eyes a shining black. His name was Bear Heart.

Bear Heart had flown to Tallahassee to give a talk on Native American medicine at a healing arts festival. He began his talk with an explanation of his background. He had studied under two traditional Muskogee Creek teachers, Daniel Beaver and David Lewis. Later, as his healing practice expanded, he helped people of many tribes and cultures and learned other healing techniques. At speaking engagements like this one, where he was speaking mostly to non-Indians, he sought to break through stereotypes.

"The Indian isn't just sitting around moping about the buffalo," he said. "We like to laugh and enjoy life."

At one point, he said he could send positive energy to people with just good thoughts. "Take him, for example," he said, pointing to me. "I will turn my back, and in a moment he will feel something good." He turned around and a warm, pure feeling came over me, much like what I had experienced on the Appalachian Trail.

After his talk, Bear Heart invited people to visit his healing table outside, at no charge. I had strained my neck from doing yoga, resulting in some swelling, so I took my turn in waiting for Bear Heart's help. When the time came, he had me lie down on the cot and relax. I explained the problem with my neck and also asked him about the recent presence of large hawks in my life. Their sudden appearance, both in dreams and physical reality, struck me as being more than coincidental. One such bird—an osprey—had visited me outside the pizza business where I was working. It was a raptor I thought to be a large kite at first, hovering thirty feet overhead.

"They are good messengers," Bear Heart told me. "The hawk may some day give you a vision and even the power to heal people."

He began chanting softly, intermittently blowing short, rapid breaths over my body. He then concentrated on my neck, blowing and waving a fan of flicker feathers. Closing my eyes, I began to feel lighter, as if in a dream. In my mind's eye, I was merging with something bright, warm, and wonderful. I sat up and began flapping my arms as if they were wings. Bear Heart chuckled. "I took you flying over the Appalachians," he later told me, even though I had never mentioned my Appalachian Trail hike. I felt my neck, and it was healed.

Later that year, I had a brief phone conversation with Bear Heart. "I'm heading west in a couple of weeks," I began hesitantly, "and wondered if I could stop in to see you."

Since the healing arts festival, Bear Heart had visited Tallahassee on one other occasion, and we had made a stronger connection. Being a sincere seeker, I wanted to learn more. Bear Heart was a busy man, I knew. He was in constant demand for his services, so I didn't know what to expect.

"There is a ceremony," he said in his deep voice, "the Southern Cheyenne Sun Dance. It lasts for four days, and it starts in a week."

"How do I find it?"

He told me the name of a small Oklahoma town. "Just drive there and ask any Indian," he said abruptly. "I'll see you there." Click . . .

My previous phone calls to Bear Heart had focused on helping people in Tallahassee. The most challenging experience had been in supporting a mutual friend in his efforts to break free from the grips of an evil influence. During the episode, it became apparent that Bear Heart could send healing energy long distances; much of his guidance took place on a psychic plane. He challenged me to use faculties I was unaccustomed to using. Certain situations, I realized, had been set up as tests and learning experiences. And now I was to drive to a small Oklahoma town and somehow find the sun dance? Excitement mixed with nervousness. I had never been around large groups of Native Americans and doubted that many non-Indians would be at the ceremony.

A history book gave me some information about the Cheyenne, but little about the sun dance. The earliest known recorded evidence of the Cheyenne and Arapaho people was around AD 1600. Being of Algonquian linguistic stock, the Arapaho lived around the headwaters of the Mississippi River in what is present-day northern Minnesota, while the Cheyenne were found along the Mississippi's east bank in southern Minnesota. They farmed and hunted and lived in bark or earth-covered lodges.

Using dog travois to haul their goods, the tribes joined and slowly migrated west into the Dakotas, adopting the horse by 1800. Around 1835, a portion of the tribe separated and settled along the Arkansas River in Colorado. Several wars and massacres followed, including the infamous Sand Creek Massacre in 1868, when Colonel George Armstrong Custer attacked Chief Black Kettle's peaceful Cheyenne village. The army soon forced the Southern Cheyenne and the Arapaho to resettle in Oklahoma.

In 1877, a group of 972 Northern Cheyenne were also escorted to Oklahoma from Montana. The following year, some of these Cheyenne broke away and returned to Montana, pursued by thousands of soldiers and volunteers. Through sacrifice and determination, they remained in Montana, and a reservation was established a few years later.

After a three-day drive, I found that the town of the supposed Southern Cheyenne Sun Dance was little more than a cluster of gas stations and mini-marts. When I asked a non-Indian shopkeeper about the dance location, he looked at me as if I were an alien. Native Americans were nowhere to be seen. Obviously, this was another test. I was to find the sun dance by intuition.

Choosing a direction—north—I drove on a small highway through rolling hills and farmland. I soon stopped at an overlook and stepped out, facing west. It felt good to face that direction. Something beyond a distant row of trees pulled at me. I got back in the car and followed a dirt road that angled west, then turned onto another road dusty from traffic. Rounding a bend, I saw tents, teepees, and vehicles situated around a large field. Feeling awestruck, I pulled in and parked. When I stepped out of the car, Bear Heart's unmistakable deep voice bellowed: "Welcome! You finally made it. Get to know everyone."

I scanned the open field in the direction of his voice, but Bear Heart was nowhere to be seen. I did see Cheyenne of all ages milling about; some of them looked at me strangely, but it was obvious that no one else had heard the voice. I felt like the character in a movie who is the only one in a crowd that can hear or see the ghost or angel.

Other vehicles pulled in, and more tents were being erected. A stand sold food and beverages, one of the main features being fry bread. Children laughed and ran about, all of them dark skinned and dark haired. I drew curious glances with my brown hair, beard, and only moderate suntan—not to mention my orange Volkswagen Beetle with a Florida tag. No other VW's or non-Indian-looking people were in the entire encampment. I felt awkward and shy.

In the field I approached some elders who were setting up a huge teepee, larger than any of the others. "Have you seen Bear Heart?" I asked. They spoke to each other in Cheyenne.

"No, we haven't," one of them replied in English; then they continued talking in Cheyenne. Not knowing how to break the ice with these people except to ask about Bear Heart, I resumed my search, but with no luck. I withdrew to my VW refuge and drove to a small overlook. Farms, roads, trees, and the Canadian River stretched before me. Still feeling strong energy from the camp, I gave myself a good talk. Not only would I be a patient visitor respectful of native ways, but, more importantly, I would be myself. Just as I had come to know African-American people in the South, I would seek to establish friendships with Native Americans.

I returned and wandered around some more. Several children ran up and shot me with cap pistols. "We got you!" they cried. They were playing cowboys and Indians, and I was an obvious candidate to be a cowboy. They laughed and wondered aloud who I was. We began talking. Soon, as if I were a lost sparrow, they took me in hand and introduced me to grandfathers and grandmothers, aunts and uncles. Some children were claiming to have five or six grandparents. At first I was confused as to how this could be, until I realized that adoption was common, even if one's biological parents or grandparents were still living. In return for the children's hospitality, I allowed them to use my car as a playground.

That night, I took my entourage of children to meet an adult Cheyenne whom I had met earlier setting up a teepee. With the owner's permission, I took the smallest boy, one about four years old, inside it. "I dreamed this!" the child suddenly cried, "I dreamed you were taking me in here! I've never been in a teepee before." As he gazed wondrously at stars through the gap of the teepee chimney, the gap in his front teeth showed. How strange, it seemed, that an outsider would be the one to show a Cheyenne child his people's traditional type of lodge for the first time.

Once I was in the field again, another boy told me why he had been attracted to me in the first place. "You look like someone I know," he said. Then he whispered in my ear, "Jesus." It must have been my beard and moderately long hair. Those whiskers came in handy for something.

When the children had returned to their camps, I talked with the teepee's owner, a big man with an easy laugh, whom I shall call Charlie. He was an alcoholism counselor who worked with people of many tribes. The alcoholism rate among his people was 60 to 80 percent among adults, and he had no illusions about how difficult such a trend is to reverse. Charlie had been on the recovery path himself. I asked if traditions such as the sun dance helped to restore pride and fight alcoholism. His answer surprised me.

"A preacher once told me," he began, lowering his voice, "that God comes through nature and the sun-dance pole because He feels sorry for the Indians." Charlie regularly attended the Christian church, but he had never danced in the sun-dance ritual. He said it was extremely rigorous, especially the fasting for four days without food or water to show commitment to the tribe and to the Great Spirit.

"What's going to happen?" I asked, my knowledge limited to an occasional book passage and photograph and from hearing Bear Heart talk.

Charlie gave me a broad grin. He may not have been a sun dancer, but he knew the ways of his people. "Oh, you will find out!" he laughed. Nervously, I laughed with him.

Charlie then gave me a beautifully beaded watchband his wife had made for him. I gracefully accepted it, even though I had lost my watch earlier that same day. Later, I wondered about the symbolism of having received the traditionally designed band so soon after I had lost the watch I could have put it on. Perhaps the modern and the traditional worlds were not quite complementary, at least for the duration of the sun dance. After all, for how many centuries had this ceremony been observed before the first timepiece reached the Great Plains?

A speaker called people to a large teepee along the circular clearing where sun dancers were about to rehearse. A circle of men pounded a huge drum and began singing in high-pitched voices as dancers blew eagle-bone whistles in unison while bobbing up and down. Women in the outlying circle sang with the men, usually ending a song by singing one chorus on their own after the drumming stopped.

Bear Heart had described how the sun dance was performed for renewal and creation, it being believed that the dancers generated energies that were sent through the entire universe. The roles of both males and females were vitally important to this purpose. Women as cocreators of life are believed to be representative of Mother Earth. They, too, danced to the ceremonial drum, but their movements were different from those of the men, being more of a gentle dipping motion with their feet rarely leaving the ground, and they did not blow on the whistles. As the dancing continued, I remembered what Bear Heart had said about the drum: It represented the heartbeat of Mother Earth—or maybe it *was* the heartbeat, became the heartbeat.

Correspondingly, perhaps the male dancers and their whistles were representative of the upper world, or Father Spirit.

My gaze wandered to the silhouette of teepee poles against a star-filled sky. I glimpsed how the Cheyenne had lived a hundred or more years ago—in circular villages surrounded by vast, unspoiled country, where the whistles and songs of sun dancers had mingled with those of snorting bison and peeping prairie dogs.

In the East, near Tallahassee, I once searched for a ceremonial grounds used by generations of Creek Indians, wanting to sense the energy of the area and the people and to visualize the dances and ceremonies that must have occurred there. I never found it. The grounds had disappeared—which now impressed me as all the more reason for the still-living Cheyenne Sun Dance.

The sun dancers practiced long into the night. I slept on a small rise overlooking the encampment, the rhythm and music of the drums and singing reverberating in my head. It seemed to rekindle something deep inside. Somehow, I knew the Cheyenne and the sun dance. It is the kind of knowing that is difficult to wrap words around, like a vague memory or smell from early childhood. At the same time, I felt like a white duckling in a flock of brown geese. I looked different, acted different, and perhaps thought and dreamed differently. Why had I come?

The next morning, a crier called the young men to clear the main circle of trash and brush. I felt moved to join. No one objected. Immediately, I hoisted up a charred wooden cross from the tall grass, feeling as though I had found a corpse. An elder hurried over and said it had been left by the Ku Klux Klan a couple of weeks before. He said they had also tried to burn the central sun-dance pole from the previous year. "If we find them, we scalp them!" he said with a faint smile. White racists in the South have advocated sending minorities back to their original homelands, but where would they send Native Americans?

Another man told me that the KKK, some drunks, or both had perpetrated the desecration. In any case, such an act was like that of writing graffiti on the Sistine Chapel. Respect was the primary code at the sun-dance grounds. No alcohol or drugs were allowed, and neither were cameras, sketchbooks, or, in the immediate circle, food or water. Elders and tribal police enforced the policies and minimized disruptions.

Earlier, I had talked with a tribal policeman who was an uncle of one of the children. He said there were only five tribal patrol cars to cover an eight-county area. Since Oklahoma had no established reservations, the areas on the map owned predominately by Native Americans were simply labeled "Indian land." The tribal police, funded by the Bureau of Indian Affairs, had jurisdiction over these Indian areas if called upon by the Native Americans themselves or by local police officers. The officer said that the native way of dealing with problems often differed from methods employed by the dominant culture; for that reason, the tribal police had special training.

When I dutifully hauled the burnt cross to the trash pile, the elder in charge of the young men walked over and told me the legend of how Sweet Medicine, an early Cheyenne prophet, had gone into a cave near Bear Butte, South Dakota, and met with the spirits of four races. He had then returned to the tribe with sacred arrows and a message of a new sacred dance to be performed—the sun dance. After telling me this story, the elder looked at me thoughtfully. "It used to be that people weren't coming to the sun dance any more; just the older ones would show up. But I feel good at seeing a lot of young ones this year. There are more people here this year than in any other I can remember."

The elder walked on as if he had said enough. I was beginning to learn that one did not ask questions. Instead, the elders seemed to have an intuitive sense of what one sought or needed, and they presented it in their own way.

The sun-dance priest emerged from the main teepee and asked the young workers, including me, to sit in a half circle facing the lodge. He was middle aged, I guessed, and appeared fatigued, though grounded. "I have talked with your ancestors," he said loudly. Then, looking straight at me, he added, "All of them!" I shivered. We filed into the teepee. The priest selected one of many pipes and showed us how to smoke it, taking four puffs. We passed it among us. The oldest man in the lodge, thin and almost bald, gave a prayer of protection in Cheyenne, for we were about to be sent to retrieve the sun-dance lodge poles and the main center pole.

It was hot, hard work hauling cottonwood trees from damp bottomlands. The property was managed by the Army Corps of Engineers, from whom the Cheyenne had obtained permission to cut the logs. An elder had already done the selecting, each log having to meet certain specifications. The main center pole was the most important. It was a fat cottonwood with a large fork that began at about thirty feet high. The trees were heavy and the ground muddy; teamwork was a necessity.

The elder had been selecting sun-dance poles for more than ten years. He had danced the year before, even though he was well over seventy years of age. The only time I saw him frown was when he learned that one of the tribe's chain saws was still at a man's house instead of being where it was needed.

"It is the tribe's," the elder said firmly. "The chain saw belongs to the *tribe.*" Those words lingered in my ears. I could only imagine the difficulty of keeping a tribe together in modern times. Tribal members were spread over several towns, cities, and states. The only designated Cheyenne reservation belonged to the Northern Cheyenne in Montana. Central activities such as the sun dance, though, helped to bind the tribe together. Later, as if to make that point, the keeper of the missing chain saw appeared with it and put it to good use.

In the old days, the sun dance would have been held in close proximity to where the poles were cut, so that they could be easily dragged to the dance site. The present site, however, was miles away, and so we loaded the poles onto a tractor trailer bed.

Upon returning to camp, the young men were asked to split into four clans at the main circle. They were to have a foot race and other activities to help initiate the main pole. I wanted to join them, but I had no clan. I retreated to the outskirts, my sense of anomie returning.

I awoke hours before dawn. Without my missing watch, I couldn't be sure, but it seemed to be around two or three a.m. I sensed the presence of the sun-dance priest; his spirit seemed to be nudging me awake. Just then, the crier called for the people to come. It was time to erect the center sun-dance pole and lodge.

Sleepily, I walked past tents and teepees toward the main circle, where the huge center pole lay on the ground. A young Indian man stopped me, saying, "Hey, man, I don't think you should be here!"

My anticipation sank. A moment later, from some thirty yards away (well out of earshot), the sun-dance priest announced, "Everyone can help!" Then an elder assistant ran over to me and said with a smile, "That means you, too, Whiskers. You're here for a reason!"

The young man slunk away. I could understand how he felt. He didn't want the sun dance overrun with visitors, especially non-Indians. But on the other hand, the ceremony had become a spiritual magnet for me. I had worked and sweated alongside the Cheyenne in anticipation of this moment. I surged forward with the rest.

Exhilarated, I joined a line of other young men. We grabbed a thick rope and pulled the huge log toward a deep hole. On the fourth tug—the elders insisted we do it in four tugs—we slid the tree into its slot and hoisted it erect. There was a loud *thunk*; the now upright fork resembled a pair of outstretched hands cupping the sky. A quiet awe filled the air; the pole stood against a blanket of stars—the center of our universe.

Maybe this was what raising the boulders at Stonehenge had been like—the earth's children coming together in spiritual unity, becoming a force in creation. In seeing the upright center pole, it was easy to feel as if I were part of the Cheyenne and of every other tribe, living and extinct. I felt the earth as a living being and this sacred spot as one of her birth canals through which energy and love poured forth.

We built the horizontal framework of a circular lodge around the pole and then fit one end of several straight poles into the center pole's fork to serve as rafters. With so many people working in unison, the lodge was quickly erected. Sheets and tarps were laid over it to help shade dancers from the hot sun later in the day. Aromatic sage was then spread across the lodge floor, and a small altar was built around a buffalo skull.

With preparations complete, the drummers readied themselves. Dancers filed in, and the full sun dance began. Inside and outside the newly erected lodge, people focused energy on the main pole, the sacred vessel or tree of life through which the Creator would communicate. As the deep drumming and high-pitched singing intensified, I felt a strong sense of belonging, of homecoming, even. How, I wondered, could an entire society—all of Western culture—so greatly distance itself from ceremonies that celebrated the earth?

It was at this point that I saw Bear Heart for the first time. He was serving as a "painter" for a dancer, meaning that he painted the dancer's body with different colors and symbols and assisted in other ways. Bear Heart had danced in Cheyenne Sun Dances at eight different times, twice the usual pledge, and he now assisted other dancers.

When the dancing ended for the evening, I spoke with him. "I heard you were here," he said. "Where have you been?" He asked as if he already knew the answer.

"Oh, around," I answered sheepishly.

"Get your things and camp with us."

He introduced me to his wife, Edna, and to Mary, a non-Indian friend. I presented him with a handwoven Navajo-style blanket and some tobacco, and he seemed pleased.

Late in the night (or possibly early in the morning), the dancers reassembled. I suddenly realized why I had lost my watch. Its loss symbolized that I had left the secular realm where things took place according to the clock. In the sacred realm of the ceremony, the dance would begin and end, not at any specific time, but only when the energy was right.

As I was sitting behind the circle of dancers with the stars overhead, it seemed that all the spirits of the Cheyenne nation had been called forth, and of other nations as well. Spirits emerged beside and above me—tingly, pulling, faces smiling—welcoming. They knew me. I felt I knew them. Images of a beautiful land of lakes and northern woods filled my mind's eye, perhaps the home of the Cheyenne before they emerged on the Plains, or perhaps the home of my Iroquois ancestors, or both. Tribal bonds of long ago spoke to me. No time or cultural divide separated us. The Europeans had never arrived; the land was pure and wild. Our common link was through the Great Spirit and the pure vessel of the sun-dance pole.

The day and dance progressed and, unbelievably, the energy kept building. The dancers' families entered the lodge and placed dishes of food before them. The painters' families then went in and brought out the food, using it for their own meals. It was a gift for the painters' help. It must have been tempting for the dancers, after having gone for days without food or water, to gaze upon the large juicy watermelons and other treats—just another one of their many tests.

I felt honored when Bear Heart asked that I join his family in bringing out the food that had been offered to him. It was an equal honor to enter the sacred lodge at those times. During these intervals, elders and dancers spoke to the tribe, relaying personal pledges and other messages.

One elderly man was finishing a pledge for a son who had died two years before. The early death had prevented the son from fulfilling the normal pledge to dance in the ceremony at least four times in a lifetime, and so the father was doing it for him. Another dancer began by saying, "I do not speak English very well. I am a sick man who has spoken Cheyenne all his life. But many of the young people do not learn Cheyenne, and so I will speak English." The man had a dual message: to be understood by the young people, he had to speak English, but he was saddened that his native tongue was not being learned or spoken as much.

As the sun approached its zenith, the singing and drumming reached a crescendo. Dancers suddenly left the lodge and reentered from each of the four directions. Finally, they stood once more in the center, blowing their whistles until family members grabbed them. The physical dance was over—while the spiritual dance spiraled on.

Upon reaching camp, Bear Heart placed a striking green, blue, and red Pendleton blanket over my shoulders. "You are now my nephew," he announced. We hugged, my heart swelling. "You have also inherited many relatives."

An elder Cheyenne woman approached. Wisps of gray streaked her long hair; she bore a young smile. "This is my Cheyenne mother," said Bear Heart. I knew immediately he meant his adopted mother. "She is now your grandmother." The woman nodded and smiled; I felt total acceptance.

Her son came over, another new uncle whom I shall call Stiff Leg because of his limp. We began talking. He told me that Taos, New Mexico, was a place I should visit. A large native population lived there, along with numerous seekers like me. He asked if I could take him there. I surprised myself at how quickly I agreed. Bear Heart seemed fine with the idea and asked that I stay with him on my way back east.

My departure occasioned many hugs and tears. The previous four days would live forever in my heart. While I had faced challenges in coming to the sun dance, I knew Bear Heart had also been challenged by inviting me to a ceremony not open to the general public. He was serving as a bridge for me to learn about Native American cultures, opening pathways of understanding and enlightenment. In the eyes of some Native Americans, it was a controversial role for him to fill.

As my new Cheyenne uncle and I drove off, the evening grew surprisingly cold, my VW having no working heater. I wrapped my new Pendleton blanket over our legs while we peered into the Oklahoma night, heading west.

Chapter

3

TAOS TEACHINGS

"You now, I'm sitting right next to you, but you ignore me," Stiff Leg complained gruffly as we drove to Taos. As usual, my mind had been wandering while I drove. "When you thought I was sleeping a little while ago, I was really trying to figure you out," Stiff Leg went on. "I think you're too much up here [he tapped my head] and not enough here [he tapped my heart]."

Stiff Leg did not mince words. "You are just a baby," he said. "You have much to learn about our ways." Then, as if to humble me further, he added, "If you have something to teach me, I will follow you all the way to Florida!"

He let that sink in for a moment; then he softened. "I have helped many guys like you learn our ways. I am a Cheyenne dog soldier, but I was also the first hippie." He smiled. I glanced at him and smiled back. Even though his observations of me were a bit unorthodox, he meant them to be constructive.

By example, Stiff Leg was teaching me something else: how to endure discomfort. Volkswagen Beetles are not engineered for tall, angular people with debilitating leg and hip injuries, his having been the result of a car accident. Stiff Leg's chiseled brown face often winced with pain, especially when he got in and out of the car, but he never uttered a complaint. He was, after all, a dog soldier.

Once in Taos, Stiff Leg set out to prove his claim of being "the first hippie." He gave me a tour through non-Indian, alternative communities based on native teachings, places that had been labeled "hippie communes" just a few years before. Some had built pueblo-style structures and kiva-like communal rooms. One community, though, was raising healthy looking marijuana plants in their green-house—not exactly an ancient staple.

Next on our tour was the main architectural model for the modern communes—Taos Pueblo, impressively perched before the sacred Taos Mountain. These were some of the oldest two- and three-story apartment complexes in the New World; dusty streets stretched in a myriad of directions, reminiscent of contemporary downtown hubs. Fascinated, I separated from Stiff Leg just as, when a child, I used to do from my mother when she took me to malls and department stores.

I soon found myself on a seemingly abandoned dirt street. Dusty dogs wandered about, paying little attention to me. The only people I saw were two small figures hunched beside a building. They appeared to be a young boy and girl. Upon seeing me, the girl let out a small cry, and the boy took her in his arms and shielded her face. "You are not supposed to be in this area," he told me sternly.

Mystified, I apologized and backtracked. I had not seen a sign forbidding visitors to enter. Moreover, these "children" seemed very old, yet they did not have the usual body structure of human dwarfs.

Later, when I related the story to Stiff Leg, he said he thought he knew who they were, but he did not elaborate. It was just another mystery for me to ponder.

Around sunset, Stiff Leg guided me to the Rio Grande Valley outside of town. Soon, we were sitting around a fire with several Native Americans and non-Indians. Each took a turn singing and drumming Native American peyote chants. Having worshipped with each other for several years, they displayed a camaraderie I enjoyed.

The peyote drumbeat was fast paced, with each song seeming to have the same rhythm. The high-pitched singing consisted of a series of syllables and words strung together in rapid-fire succession. The intensity of this music would help keep one awake during the all-night peyote meetings.

I leaned over and asked my uncle if I could learn how to sing peyote songs. He scoffed. "You've been here only a little while and you want to learn to sing? That's not how it's done. You are only a baby." He also ridiculed me for asking too many questions in the circle. Questions and answers were not the Indian way, he said.

After the singing, my uncle and I visited the house of two Indian men in Taos. To my dismay, they opened a whiskey bottle and began passing it. Hours passed. They didn't sleep or allow me to sleep. I refused to drink and was fortunate that they didn't force the alcohol down my throat. The drinkers, I found, felt uneasy around non-drinkers, as if there were an inequality that needed leveling.

One man, whom I shall call Fred, said the rent was due the next day and he needed to get busy with some silversmithing, but he didn't move. At around dawn, he began speaking earnestly about his traditional pueblo village. Suddenly, he turned to me, "Will you take me to see my parents? I haven't seen them in weeks!"

An alarm went off in my head. I remembered a night in high school when I had been partying with friends and a guy had suddenly blurted, "Hey, let's go to Disney World! I haven't been to Disney World yet." Despite the fact that it had been midnight and Orlando was six hours away, we had piled into his VW bus and driven all night. It was dawn when we passed through the gates of the surreal "Magic Kingdom," a strange place even when one is perfectly sober and well rested. After our journey, the jingle "It's a Small World" had echoed in my head for days, a post-traumatic hangover from Mickey and Friends.

"Will you take me to see my parents?" Fred was asking again. The other two joined in his request.

"But you're drinking," I protested. "Your parents won't want to see you like this." I wasn't just making excuses. Intuitively, I felt the timing of such a visit wasn't right. Even a "baby" can think clearly.

"It is fine," he insisted. "Will you take me to see my parents?"

I sighed. "How far is it?"

Stiff Leg frowned. "That doesn't matter," he said sternly. "Just say 'yes.'"

Feeling like a juvenile snipe hunter holding a flashlight and gunnysack, I reluctantly agreed. With dawn's rays shooting over the mesa tops, we embarked for the pueblo village where Fred's parents lived. A sign indicated that it was more than seventy miles away. For some reason, I knew we would not see Fred's parents. Even my car seemed to sense something was amiss. It backfired most of the way. Vintage VW bugs were not equipped with computerized ignition timing that adjusted to elevational changes. I frequently had to stop the car, open the back hood, and move the distributor to adjust the timing. Improvements were only temporary.

When we pulled into Fred's village, the car was jerking and backfiring. I worried about first impressions. Custer had had the same problem.

Fred's village was divided into two sections. One contained more recently built structures with electric lines running to them, while the other was older and more traditional, without electricity. Fred's parents lived in the older section. As we approached his dirt street, a large black-and-white sign blocked the road: NO NON-INDIANS ALLOWED BEYOND THIS POINT. Evidently, private summer ceremonies were occurring.

"You guys go ahead," I said. "I'm basically non-Indian. I'll wait in the car."

To my astonishment, Fred didn't budge. He sat quietly, frowning. "No," he finally said. "If you can't go in, none of us will." The others agreed. "This is not our peoples' way," he continued. "We once had a light-skinned prophet visit us long ago, and these ceremonies are supposed to be open to anyone in case he comes back. Besides, maybe you're right; my mother shouldn't see me like this." I was filled with a sudden sense of admiration. Even while he was drinking, some of Fred's strongest values had shone through.

We turned around and headed back toward Taos. I was intrigued by the prophet story and impressed with Fred's insistence on the "all-for-one" principle. I soon became discouraged, however, when the same principle was used to cajole me into buying them a bottle of wine and some food. Besides having the only vehicle, albeit an imperfect one, I now ascertained that I was the only one with any cash. How could I have fallen into such a situation? If they hit me up for the rent—and I expected that request to be forthcoming—my VW would only be good for sleeping in, as I would have no money with which to get home.

"Uncle, I think it is time for me to move on," I said when our bleary-eyed group reached Taos.

"No!" he said sternly, "I have one more place to show you." Reluctantly, I agreed to stay a few more hours. We left our two friends and caught up on sleep under a shady cottonwood in the local park. We were not alone. The park was a regular outdoor hotel, and free. Winos and binge drinkers were plentiful and stretched out in every imaginable position. If only Georgia O'Keefe had painted that scene!

In late afternoon, we awoke and Stiff Leg took me to his last promised stop, a large adobe home of an artist friend of his. We sat in a glassed-in porch and sipped tea, viewed paintings, and counseled the artist about his "painter's block." My uncle handed him a small bag. It was peyote. "Here, this will help you," he assured him.

I was beginning to wonder why I was there when my uncle pointed out the clear glass that covered the ceiling and the house's southern exposure. "Solar energy in winter," he said with a satisfied smile. "Heats up the whole house."

Indeed, I had a keen interest in such things, although I had never told him so.

We parted with a hug. "Stay in your heart, nephew," he said, tearfully. "You're still just a baby." He paused and then added, "Could you give me a twenty?"

HONOR

With a bruised spirit and a lighter billfold, I made my way back to Oklahoma. "Now you have seen the not-so-good side of us," Bear Heart announced when I arrived at his house. "Stiff Leg once saw me put hot coals in my mouth as part of a healing practice. The coals don't burn me when I do it properly. I saw him a few weeks afterward and he had burns all around his mouth. Could hardly talk. He wouldn't tell me how it happened, but I found out later he was showing off in a bar by trying to use the hot coals. It didn't work for him."

As we sat in Bear Heart's living room, he made a quick call and a native woman soon arrived with two large spotted eagle feathers. "They have been handed down in my family for many years," she said. Bear Heart had me look them over. He gave the woman some money for one I thought was exceptional. When she left, he allowed me to examine the feathers of the anhinga bird and others he kept in his medicine box—tools of his trade. Bear Heart claimed that, in using the feathers for healing, he communicated about their purpose with the bird's spirit.

Soon, Bear Heart led me to a hilly, forested area east of Oklahoma City, where he had me stay with his friend Mary, whom I had met at the sun dance. He began my introduction to his country retreat by chanting and pounding a drum in the living room. In my mind's eye, I saw him point to approaching spirits who flew on wings. These were guardians of the area, I surmised. They helped me feel relaxed and comforted.

"This is where I come to get away from the city and recharge my batteries," Bear Heart said when he finished drumming. "The little people are very strong here." He paused and looked at me intently, as if to ascertain whether I was ready to hear more. Then he continued, "A long time ago, my people made an agreement with the little people to work together, and we've been connected ever since. I work with them often, especially in protecting a person or house. They can even kill a person if they wish, but they won't."

"They get into the cupboards sometimes," added Mary, "and move things all over the floor. They are mischievous, but they mean no harm."

I gathered that the "little people"—what the Creeks call the *isti-lah-bugs-chee* or *stee-la-booch-go-gee*—were nature spirits or fairies, something I once thought were reserved for Irish folk tales or the Findhorn Garden in Scotland. But Bear Heart would tell me nothing more about them before he left for the evening.

That night, to my complete surprise, I experienced the little people firsthand. While I was trying to sleep, several luminescent childlike beings about the size of three-year-olds entered my room. They climbed on my back and literally rolled me back and forth on the bed, squealing with high-pitched laughter. They also rolled with each other on the floor in playful wrestling.

Dumbstruck, I didn't know whether to wrestle with them, cry for help, or simply lay there and pretend it wasn't happening. Remembering what Bear Heart had told me about their power, and also an earlier recommendation of what to do if cornered by a grizzly bear, I decided to lay there and let them pounce on me as if I were their big brother. This they did exuberantly. In no way were they hurting me, however. I felt intrigued, awed, humored, and honored, all at the same time.

My only previous similar experience had occurred a couple of years earlier in the southern Appalachian Mountains. It had been midwinter, and I was solo backpacking along the remote Chattooga River. Just before sunset I set up camp, started a fire, and went to the river for water. Suddenly, a large, booming sound echoed through the valley, immediately followed by a huge splash in the middle of the river, as if a boulder had been heaved into it. On the opposite shore, several medium-sized furry creatures—smaller than bears but larger than beavers—crashed through the brush. I saw only their bodies and four legs, not their heads, and thought it odd that animals would be active in below-freezing weather. I was startled, but figured that as long as they stayed on the opposite shore, I was fine.

Returning to the river to wash dishes, I heard the same booming noise and tremendous splashes. This time, however, the furry creatures were crashing through the brush on *my* side of the river! At the time, I did not have someone like Bear Heart for a spiritual guide, nor had I read about metaphysical subjects other than what was contained in *Black Elk Speaks*. I wondered if these creatures lived on another plane most of the time, maybe under water, rarely emerging as physical beings. I wasn't in the mood to linger and find out. Haphazardly, I packed my gear and hiked back to my car, guided by the faint yellow beam of my flashlight.

Now, though, that night at Mary's in Oklahoma, it was different. I did not stray from my bed when the little people made themselves known, although sleep was not an option. The wrestling episodes occurred on and off all night.

"I called Bear Heart last night," Mary announced in the morning around the breakfast table. "Things were so charged up that I couldn't sleep."

"I'll say," I said, yawning. "Those little people were climbing all over me."

"I'll ask him to talk to their mother again," she said.

Their mother?

Mary had to work in the city, and so I was left alone to write and to slow down. During the previous year, I had come to regard Bear Heart as more than a healer; he was a way-shower who often helped me deepen my attunement with the earth and expand my mind to go beyond the intellect. Spending the day alone in a forest setting without an itinerary was a perfect prescription. Glimpsing the little people gleefully rolling around in the dirt was simply an added bonus. Later, I heard they favored strawberries. If I had known that at the time, I would have purchased a quart of ripe berries and distributed them around the yard.

The Muskogee tribe has had a long documented history with the little people. Jackson Lewis, the grandfather of one of Bear Heart's teachers, was a boy on the Trail of Tears. For the long trek from the Southeast to Oklahoma, he was given a pony to ride. Crossing the Mississippi River, suddenly he was knocked from his horse in midstream. Fortunately, he was able to grab the pony's tail. The others could only watch and pray as the horse swam and struggled against the current, towing the young boy. Afterward, many commented on seeing a little man sitting on the head of the pony, guiding his movements. It was the first time anyone had seen the little people for four generations! The event seemed to be a sign. It gave the tribe hope that the little people would help them in their new land and teach them how to use new herbs and plants for healing.

David Lewis, Jr., the great-grandson of Jackson Lewis, described his first encounter with the little people—at age seven—in his book, *Creek Indian Medicine Ways*. He had dozed off while fishing by a creek. When he awakened, a little man was watching him. "His toenails were long," Lewis recounted, "but yet his hair was well kept. His hair was long, but it wasn't dangling; it was real neat. And then he didn't have clothes, but he had a kind of bandolier of plant leaves across in front. . . . And he said, 'I'll be with you till the day you die.'"[1]

As Lewis grew older and learned the medicine ways of his people, the little man appeared to him on several occasions, often to show him healing plants. Yet his diminutive helper never seemed to grow any older.

Once, Lewis denied the existence of the little people to a preacher. That night, he was startled awake by someone yanking on his hair. "On the window sill there, that little man I had seen many years ago was sitting down, his feet hanging down," he said. "There was anger in his voice. He said, 'I'm real.' And then he said it again, 'I'm real.' Just like that. And then in a twinkle of an eye he was gone."[2]

According to Seminole spiritual leader Willie Lena, the little people take in lost children and show them how to use herbal remedies. They often play with children and talk to them. In one account, a child said the little people were packing their goods in tiny wagons because their house would soon be destroyed. Soon thereafter, a tornado leveled the grove of trees in which they lived. A similar event occurred just before a highway was cut through a forest.[3]

In describing the little people and the differences between believers and nonbelievers, traditional native people point out that many Westerners accept only facts and proof, seeing only as far as their "headlights" can reach. In contrast, "the Indian knows that he is one piece of a multidimensional world," observes Chickasaw author Robert Perry.[4]

Bear Heart and his wife, Edna, arrived at Mary's in the evening. He carefully made an outdoor fire inside a stone ring he said had been used by native people for generations. He offered tobacco to the flames and then, reaching into the fire with a bare hand, extracted a hot, glowing coal. I tried to keep my mouth from dropping open. Obviously, the blistering heat didn't bother him. It was part of his medicine. He called me over and had me face east. Then he put ash on my face and forehead. "We are giving you a more proper adoption ceremony," he announced.

He then presented me with a striking blue shirt adorned with colorful narrow ribbons, holding it up to my shoulders to ensure a proper fit. We hugged warmly. Edna gave me a beautifully woven shawl. "This is for your mother," she said. "The women wear them during many traditional dances." My heart swelled, for she had never met my mother. Mary presented me with a Pendleton blanket, welcoming me as her nephew. It was a night of many honors.

Bear Heart rekindled the sacred fire the next night. This time, he directed me to kneel on the west side of the fire, facing east. He handed me a pipe with a long wooden stem and a red bowl. "This is a sun-dance pipe," he said reverently. "Now, it is yours. It is not something I am just giving you. You've earned it. Now you can travel [astrally] without worrying about bad spirits or witches. You can help many people."

He showed me how to fill the bowl with pure tobacco mixed with other herbs. We smoked together. Prayers were sent to all four directions and to Father Spirit and Mother Earth. A deep reverence filled my entire being. I felt I was on the Appalachian Trail again, gazing out from a Maine mountaintop.

"You must never smoke while drinking," Bear Heart warned, "and don't let a woman on her menstrual cycle touch the pipe. At that time, she is going through such a strong cleansing that she could ground out the energy."

Bear Heart then opened his medicine box and held out the spotted eagle feather he had obtained the day I arrived. "I know you will help many people in Tallahassee," he said encouragingly. The feather felt warm in my hands. Tears welled in my eyes. How had I deserved such an honor?

I felt a greater responsibility to keep myself pure in order to channel healing energy through the eagle feather and the pipe.

When the fire died down and Bear Heart left, Mary told me she had been given a pipe by a medicine woman, the late Evelyn Eaton, who wrote *I Send a Voice*, among other books.[5] Mary also told me she herself often traveled as an animal spirit. And she relayed a way Bear Heart traveled: "A friend and I were sitting around a fire one night," she began, "and my friend said she felt something very big and powerful leaning over her. Later, when we looked around, we found bear paw prints in the dirt. We knew it had been Bear Heart."

"The bear spirit comes when I will it," Bear Heart said two days later. He seemed a bit embarrassed for my having brought the subject up. At the time, we were driving to western Oklahoma for a Native American Church meeting, a century-old native ceremony that blended Christianity with common tribal spiritual elements such as a sacred fire, drumming, and traditional songs. The gathering was being held in honor of a young Cheyenne man who had just graduated from high school.

I knew participants sang and prayed all night while ingesting peyote as a sacrament. Bear Heart would tell me nothing more except that when the tobacco and cornhusks were passed around, I should roll a cigarette with them and smoke a silent prayer, placing the butt on a crescent-moon altar. Otherwise, he wished for me to form my own impressions without preconceived images, which was an integral part of his teaching method.

At a small town near the meeting site, we rested and ate dinner at the home of a Cheyenne family. Bear Heart seemed deep in thought and said little.

"I need to go for a walk," I told him.

"Hmmmnn," he grunted.

I walked as Bear Heart had taught me, breathing deeply into my abdomen area while trying to stay centered. "One can walk many miles without getting tired that way," he told me. He had also shown me another exercise—that being to raise my arms over my head suddenly and powerfully, like a bear threatening an intruder. As I did so now, walking past rolling prairie grass bathed in sunset hues, I indeed felt the bear spirit. It was the spirit of an animal with keen senses, power, and curiosity. I knew this greater energy and sensitivity would help me walk for hours, if necessary. When I returned to the house, Bear Heart grunted, nodding. His glowing eyes looked almost crossed.

A short time after sunset, we entered a large teepee in a clockwise fashion. A V-shaped fire blazed before a crescent-moon sand altar. On the altar's center was a peyote button, what I later learned was called "Father Peyote." The participating men were arrayed in fine ribbon shirts and woven vests, and the women wore long, traditional dresses. All were adorned with silver and turquoise jewelry, some of which depicted the anhinga bird. Several people held fans made from the turkey-like anhinga tail feathers.

I knew the anhinga, what these worshippers called "the water bird." It is a brown-and-black bird from my area of the Southeast, sometimes called the "snake bird" because of its long, snake-like neck. An ancient species, the anhinga does not have the oil glands that ducks and other birds do to keep their wings from getting water logged, so they frequently perch on branches with their wings spread out to dry. Unlike wading birds that seek to catch fish by poking into the water from above it, the anhinga swims underwater, undulating its serpentine neck and spearing fish with a sharp bill. Then the bird surfaces, flips the impaled fish into the air, and swallows it head first. Bear Heart had told me the anhinga has a feminine energy, symbolic of Mother Earth, while birds of prey, with their more masculine energy, represent the sky realm.

In the teepee, tobacco and cornhusks were soon passed— this part Bear Heart had told me about—but beyond that lay new territory for me. Peyote soon followed in the form of a green relish and dried buttons. It was foul tasting, but I choked down a small handful. One must earn the right to learn from the peyote by enduring its bitterness and ensuing nausea, I learned later.

Bear Heart slipped me some dried peyote powder from his medicine bag. "Let it soak in your gums before swallowing it," he whispered. For my first meeting, there would be no shortage of sacrament. Fortunately, the nausea was short-lived.

A finely beaded rattle and staff were passed to begin the music; each participant took turns singing while one man drummed. The drum was a small, leather-covered iron kettle half filled with water. The tone changed every time the water was sloshed to wet the leather. The tempo never slowed. The teepee reverberated with drumming and singing—"*Ah he ya na, he na na, he ya na, we ne ne . . .*"

Occasionally, prayers were shared, ones with many tears. Who said Native Americans don't cry? All the while, white smoke spiraled out through the teepee's chimney, carrying our hopes and entreaties to the upper world.

Around midnight, drowsiness set in. I pretended to be praying, when what I really wanted to do was to catch a wink. Suddenly, my hands and feet began to move as if a drum were beating inside. I felt clear and focused. My entire being had awakened.

Gazing into the fire, I prayed for people I knew, for those in the lodge, and for the young man for whom this meeting was being held. The ceremony's leader, or the "road man," as he was called, then thanked the Creator for the many participants, including me, adding that I had been "thinking well." Many grunted approval. In such a ceremony, thoughts and prayers are powerful. At one point, I saw them rise from participants to weave a spiral of light around the teepee.

Some time in the wee hours, the road man stepped outside and blew on an eagle bone whistle four times to clear the way for us to go outside. We then took a bathroom break. In this rural setting, the stars were not dimmed by artificial lights. A million eyes seemed to peer at us. I felt that parts of me had been healing all night, as past experiences and relationships had come into focus.

The meeting went on for several more hours. Just before dawn, a woman carried a bucket and dipper of water into the lodge. She gave a long, humble prayer. She cried; many participants cried with her. This was a highlight of the ceremony. Symbolic meat, corn, and fruit soon followed—communion. Although these were Christian elements, the meeting had been dissimilar to any church service I had ever attended. Not many church congregations pray and sing all night . . . or use peyote as a sacrament.

When we finally left the teepee, incredible power rose up from the ground through my feet—dawn's greeting. We talked and joked, a change from the earlier intensity. I approached Bear Heart and an elder Cheyenne. "I've been looking at him through the fire," the elder said to Bear Heart, nodding at me. "His hand was keeping with the drum beat. That was good!" Then he turned to me, "You're not supposed to look directly at people in there. You see them through the fire. There was a guy who came in here one time, and he was going all over the place [hallucinating], but that is not what we are meant to do. If we honor and respect Grandfather Peyote, he can show us many things."

I gathered from this elder that recreational drug use was frowned upon, but when a natural substance like peyote was respectfully used in a spiritual context, it could be controlled and of benefit.

Later, I would learn about southwestern Native American stories describing the first use of peyote. They usually revolve around members of a tribe being lost from their band. The lost people wander aimlessly in the desert, desperate, until a voice invites them to eat a small cactus, promising that it will give them strength to find their way. Upon returning successfully to their tribe, the wayfaring members uphold peyote as the source of their salvation.

Eventually, ceremonies associated with the use of peyote were developed; they have been carried on in Central America since pre-Columbian times. Around 1880, for instance, a half-Comanche leader named Quanah Parker journeyed from southwestern Oklahoma to Texas to visit non-Indian relatives. He fell desperately ill. Remedies offered by his white relatives proved unsuccessful. Quanah repeatedly requested a medicine man. The family finally sent for a female *curandera*, a Mexican healer. She instructed that Quanah be laid outside on a pallet with his head to the east. She smoked tobacco over him, sang curing songs, and fed him a bitter tea made from the peyote cactus. Quanah soon recovered. The curandera showed him where the sacred cactus grew, took him to ceremonies associated with its use, and told him that since a woman had first brought peyote to the people, a woman should always have a central place in any ceremony using it.

Certain ritual objects should be used in the ceremony, the curandera further instructed: fire; incense (the Mayans used copal, but cedar would be used in North America); tobacco, in the form of cigarettes rolled in corn husks; certain birds and their feathers; peyote as the sacrament (eaten, never smoked); a central, moon-shaped altar; a "Father Peyote" button to represent the power of the belief; and a string of beads on which prayers would be counted (similar to a rosary).

When Quanah returned north, he carried with him a ceremony he believed would help his people. John Wilson, a Caddo Indian of mixed blood, also began spreading the peyote ceremony at about the same time. He incorporated more Christian influences into the ritual, perhaps reflecting his Catholic background.

Noted archaeologist James Mooney participated in several early North American peyote ceremonies and became convinced that they could help unite the tribes during the time of major transition regarding the Indian way of life.

Concerned about congressional attempts to outlaw peyote use, Mooney organized a gathering of "road men" in 1918, whereupon he helped formally to establish the Native American Church. Today, the church boasts a membership of about a quarter million. Members were heartened by a 2005 Harvard-based study finding that Navajo people who had used peyote at least one hundred times in Native American Church ceremonies scored higher on several indicators of mental health than did nonusers. When used in the ceremonial context, peyote can be an effective treatment for alcoholism, the study concluded.[6]

As Bear Heart and I drove to the noon feast at the host's house, he asked what I thought about the peyote meeting.

"I feel like I've been on a two-week backpacking trip," I replied, thinking of the memorable experiences and personal growth that had occurred in my life in just one night. Bear Heart grunted his approval. He knew what I meant.

Leaving Bear Heart the next morning was difficult, but I had environmental battles to fight at home and money to earn. Traveling had left me rich in spirit and lean in billfold. Moreover, Bear Heart had his own path to lead and other people to help heal and guide. I was thankful that our paths had crossed and hoped they would again. We parted with a hug—a great big bear hug.

THE GREATER POWER

A year had passed since the sun dance, and I was again drawn west, this time to visit Bear Heart at his new home in Albuquerque. On my way, in Oklahoma, I stayed with Cheyenne relatives I had inherited from him. My Cheyenne grandmother had suffered four heart attacks since my last visit, but she had attended the most recent sun dance and felt much better. In a ramshackle house filled with the comings and goings of people and pets, we amazingly found time and space to talk quietly.

"When the settlers first came," she said, moving a supple hand in an eastward arc, "they thought we didn't know how to pray. But we did. We'd often go high on a hill for two, maybe three, days at a time. From the woods we'd gather herbs that could heal us, and we'd always pray over them first. We knew where they came from. And the Ten Commandments—we had leaders who were already saying the same things. We were living by them."

Until the 1950s, Grandmother had lived in an encampment with other Cheyenne along a nearby river. Then the health department moved them to houses in town, citing unsanitary conditions. It seemed strange that a people who had lived on this land for millennia before the arrival of Europeans would suddenly find it illegal to live in their traditional manner.

Grandmother's old white house was easy to spot when driving down the road. A myriad of dogs, cats, and young people hung out on the porch and in the yard, as if the faded paint and sparse lawn were magnetized, drawing in life forms. Inside, the refrigerator was opened by anyone, friend or family member. At night, sleeping bodies lay strewn across floors and couches. "My father always said that if a hungry person comes to your door, feed him," Grandmother said.

Everyone pitched in to buy food, or the town grocer donated it. Grandmother's grandsons worked part-time in a government job program, or they helped nearby farmers harvest crops. One of my aunts was a schoolteacher; another was in the army. The family was adapting to the dominant culture. Grandmother was both proud and worried about their adjustment. "Maybe a time will come when our ways will be lost," she lamented. Remembering the throngs of young people at the sun dance, I knew some traditions would stand strong, at least in the current generation. Ceremonies like the sun dance were still relevant in people's lives.

The next day I drove to Albuquerque and followed the directions to Bear Heart's house. There was to be no mysterious meeting place or ceremony; I was only going to see Bear Heart and his family on their home turf. Bear Heart spent much of the day doing everyday things such as yard work and errands. Even spiritual teachers mow the lawn. Occasionally, people—both Indian and non-Indian—came seeking help. Late in the evening, when the house was quiet, Bear Heart talked about medicine.

"There was a time when we could only treat and share with our own people," he said, "but some of our prophecies spoke of a time when the sons and daughters of the conquerors would begin to wear beads and dress like us. This would begin a time of great sharing among the races. So when we saw the hippies, we knew they were a sign.

"To learn all of my ways," he continued, "you'd have to learn my language. All of my healing chants are in Muskogee. You don't have to do that. Your very presence can heal. Meditation can be the common denominator where we meet." I sensed that this message held true for other seekers as well as for me. Learning a language and culture would take years; I would basically have to move in with Bear Heart, which was impractical for both of us.

Meditating that night, I felt the truth of Bear Heart's words as my spirit seemed to swim in his glowing eyes. It seemed we flew together, visiting people who were sick and showering them with light.

Later that week, I called a friend who had recently moved to Albuquerque. He invited me to join some people on an evening cable-car trip to the summit of a nearby mountain, to be followed by an eight-mile descent by foot under a full moon. Bear Heart nodded and grunted at the idea—his way of showing approval.

Hours later, walking with my friend's group down a rocky, moonlit path, I sensed Bear Heart's presence. He seemed to be pulling me, lifting me. My spirit felt lighter with each step. Pausing, I closed my eyes and let go. I flew to peaks and outcrops above, experiencing a tremendous sense of freedom. Bear Heart was with me. We jumped from one peak to the next. I could actually experience this incredible leap-frogging while my body continued walking down the path.

Finally, we paused on an outcrop and faced northwest. The boulder-strewn view before us opened to include an expanse much broader than the surrounding valleys and peaks; the entire northwestern part of the continent glowed in a luminescent light. Time began to roll back thousands of years to an age when no human beings had lived in the immense land, not even Native Americans. Gradually, I saw a small number of people with hair completely covering their bodies walk across what I assumed to be the Bering Strait. These mysterious people scattered into the mountains.

The hairy people were followed by large migrations of people coming in different groups or tribes. They more closely resembled native people of today. My vision of their migration across the land bridge between Asia and North America was in accord with theories as to the origins of many native people. I better understood the link Bear Heart felt with other traditions and cultures, such as those found in China and India. Even certain Native American languages were closely linked to those in Asian cultures, he had said.

And, at some point, all people share common roots, roots intimately connected to Mother Earth. Perhaps this is why so many non-Indians are attracted to Native American ways. They touch something deep inside, something familiar. They help one travel to the Source for truth.

As my three-hour hike neared its end, I understood why spiritual people lose their fear of death. There is freedom in being unencumbered by the body. One could even look forward to the transition of death, if the time has come when the body is weighed down with suffering and one's purpose on earth is fulfilled. "Before you can have the Great Power," Bear Heart told me around his kitchen table late the next evening, "you must have that dependency on God, that surrendering. Then you can get into the realm of no limitations.

"Through one molecule, one can transport anywhere, sometimes to more than one place at a time. It's like a photograph transmitted by wire. People see you in flesh and blood, though your real body may be elsewhere. Some masters in one part of India can do this today.

"There is a Tibetan master I know," Bear Heart continued. "He and I communicate with each other through our minds."

Other Native Americans such as the Hopi, in fact, believe that the land from which they originally came may have been East India. "Recently, an East Indian teacher visited the Hopi to compare notes," Bear Heart said. "They found many similarities, fulfilling one of their prophecies. There are many prophecies among the various tribes. There is a belief that the buffalo represents the earth and that, today, the buffalo is standing on its last leg. It is growing bald and beginning to totter. . . . We need to establish a network of love around the world to reverse this trend."

Bear Heart invited me to travel with his family to the Four Corners area in northwestern New Mexico to visit his sister-in-law. Although our hostess did not smoke cigarettes, she had a lung cancer normally found in smokers. Most likely, the culprit was directly across the valley—a series of coal-fired power plants that billowed such thick brown smoke that the pollution was visible to orbiting astronauts.

Other environmental threats also plagued the area. Coal and uranium mining have scarred Black Mesa, three tabletop mountains that extend nearly sixty miles into the Arizona desert. Traditional Hopi Indians regard Black Mesa as the home and heart of Mother Earth. One of their ancestral instructions from the Creator tells them to keep the area pure—to not take its wealth as long as there is war. Thus, traditional Hopis oppose mining, claiming that the planet's harmonious balance is being detrimentally affected.

To help me get a better feel for the Four Corners, Bear Heart dropped me off at the nearby "Aztec Ruins," the name a misnomer for an ancient Anasazi city that flourished in the eleventh century. Since few signs of warfare were apparent in their culture, a long drought was likely what dispersed them. The former inhabitants were believed to have founded later Hopi or Pueblo villages.

I peered through small windows and ancient adobe apartments. "Some people can still hear the old songs there," Bear Heart had told me before he left. I didn't hear singing, but I soon saw a glowing, white, spirit eagle in my mind's eye. It flew toward me, hovered, and showered me with light. Bear Heart had said that such birds were often guardians of areas; they brought good messages, and one could send messages to the Creator and to others through them. "Keep yourself an open channel, an extension of the Greater Power," he had advised.

Once again, as on the moonlit trail, a part of me began

to feel light, and I let go. The spirit eagle guided me to more ancient ruins nearby—the huge dwellings of Mesa Verde, Chaco Canyon, and others. The native inhabitants still flourished as I saw them—people farming, milling corn, and playing games. I felt their peace, joy, and humble respect for the earth and the Creator.

The spirit eagle then guided me to a tabletop mesa that loomed above an unspoiled desert terrain. When I landed upon it, light and energy rose up from the earth and rock. A warm feeling swelled in my chest as light spread to stars and planets and to mountains, forests, and human inhabitants. It seemed to circle the entire universe. Some areas of the earth were starlike, reflecting the love and consciousness of the people who had settled there. I felt a kinship with native people of past and present.

Added to this strong feeling were a knowing and a seeing of how native people had once lived and of how they had changed with the arrival of the Europeans. The land was telling its own story. It was a story already known, but one I now witnessed from the vantage point of a high mesa. Change marched across the land—often violent—from east to west: wagon trails, railroads, roads, logging and mining camps, and sprawling towns and cities. Native tribes were destroyed or driven into small pockets of their original land. Yet, through the dark times, some traditional ceremonies had persevered—sun dances, sweat lodges, kachina dances, southeastern busks, and any number of other ceremonies specific to certain regions, often held in secret. One of the responsibilities of traditional Native Americans to all people, I realized, was to help maintain spiritual harmony and balance through such rituals.

I foresaw in the near future a great sharing among people of all cultures and races, a humble communion of heart and spirit moving beyond government and politics. And it would begin with one person connecting with another—as small streams join together to form a mighty river. The earth would respond by cleansing itself of waste and destruction, clearing the way for a new beginning.

For me, personally, part of my purpose was to help establish a bridge of friendship with native people, to promote healing and trust. And it would begin one step at a time.

Part

TWO

JOURNEY THROUGH
NATIVE AMERICA

Chapter

6

A NEW STEP

year and a half after my New Mexico visit with Bear
Heart, a strong image came to me as I walked
around my Tallahassee neighborhood: It was of
twenty-five to thirty people walking across California. In this unexpected vision, I knew that this group was
walking all the way to the East Coast. Their purpose was to
promote peace, ecological sanity, Native American rights,
and heart-to-heart communication. I even knew the group's
name: Walk for the Earth.

I felt good in contemplating this effort and knew that,
if I chose to take on the project, it would require months of
planning and preparation. The vision was the easy part, like
a cornerstone with walls not yet in place. The challenge was
to build the walls. This was a vision that belonged to many
people, so the first step was to share it.

That week, I spread a map of the United States across
my dining room table. The serpentine walk route jumped

out at me, glowing. The route crossed the Sierra Mountains, dipped into the Four Corners area, arched up to Lakota country, and followed the Missouri River down to Kansas City. From there, it traversed several large cities and the West Virginia Appalachians before terminating at our nation's capital. At least ten Native American reservations were crossed. Immediately, I knew this would not be a walk simply to move from west to east, but a group journey that would fully explore and experience the places and people we encountered along the way. Hopefully, we would leave behind a feeling of good will.

I soon sent letters to every known Native American nation in North America, not just to those on the walk route. Only one tribe responded. Its letter's cautious tone began, "We don't really know you. . . ." Perhaps the tribes adhered to Vine DeLoria's position in *Custer Died for Your Sins* when he advocated a "cultural leave-us-alone agreement."[1] I was likely viewed as another idealistic "wannabee," someone who has watched too many Westerns and wants to be an Indian.

On the other hand, the letters I sent to peace and conservation groups, along with the announcements I published in outdoor and environmental magazines and newsletters, generated hundreds of responses. It quickly became obvious that the walk would primarily consist of non-Indians; we had to prove our commitment to native people if doors were to open. Any amount of paper in the mail wasn't going to do it.

My efforts to solicit official endorsements and monetary contributions from large organizations or environmentally friendly companies also floundered. I wasn't a celebrity, nor was anyone else who signed up. The walk wouldn't lobby politicians or focus on key primary election states or champion a single political cause. The broad spiritual focus didn't appeal to those in corporate headquarters or on boards of directors. David Brower of Friends of the Earth, an acquaintance of mine, kindly responded to my letter by calling and basically saying, "Good luck." This would be a grassroots project, and participants would be paying for most of it out of their own pockets. I took on extra part-time jobs in order to save money for my share.

That summer, my brother Steve and I embarked on a scouting mission by car. We felt it was of primary importance to seek guidance at sacred places along the way. One such area was Bear Butte, South Dakota, a sacred mountain to Plains Indians and now a protected cultural park. Bear Heart and elders at the Cheyenne sun dance had told me about Bear Butte. Since then, I had dreamed about visiting the natural shrine, as a Muslim might be drawn to Mecca.

Steve and I arrived at Bear Butte under moonlight and laid our sleeping bags on the ground; the mountain was silhouetted against the sky. Originally, we had planned to arrive the following evening, but something prodded us forward and kept us awake at the wheel, our schedule seeming to be set forth by a Higher Power. Even at five in the morning after driving all night, sleep would not come. The earth thundered beneath me as if we were in the midst of a huge bison herd moving across the plains.

In my mind's eye, I envisioned a cave alongside the mountain. From what I had learned at the Cheyenne sun dance, this cave was where the Cheyenne prophet Sweet Medicine was given four sacred arrows by four beings of different races. From this experience, the Cheyenne had known of the black, white, and yellow races long before their arrival on the continent. Now, people of all races visit Bear Butte. They can benefit as long as they have good intent and show respect for time-honored native traditions. The belief is that pure love and light have been concentrated at Bear Butte for millennia.

Two hours later, Steve and I began a sunrise journey up the mountain. We passed a ranger who was telling tourists to stay on the trails and not to disturb or take photographs of any Native Americans they saw, who would all be there on a spiritual vigil. He acknowledged everyone warmly, his face revealing native heritage.

A crying hawk marked our path as we climbed past tobacco bags and colorful prayer flags hung in trees. Steve continued climbing while I stole away behind a boulder to smoke my pipe. The hawk kept calling and flying close. A brown furry marmot scurried down the slope beside me, seemingly unaware of my presence. Nearby lay a fluffy white down feather. Everything about the place seemed magical.

After offering pipe ashes to earth and sky, I climbed to a rocky pinnacle. A golden eagle soared below near a saddle in the mountain. Slopes and trees flickered with a strong energy field.

While the massive cathedrals of Europe need periodic renovations at great expense, the Creator continually molds Bear Butte as part of nature's grand scheme. Native people have persevered as well. Through wars, persecution, relocation, and missionary pressure, they have stubbornly persisted in seeking spiritual guidance at Bear Butte.

I met Steve on the trail, and we descended the mountain. The ranger greeted us at the parking lot, his eyes bright. "I usually don't do this," he said, "but I just feel real comfortable with you two. Come with me."

Feeling honored, we eagerly followed him away from the main trail and parking lot and descended to the base of the mountain's saddle, entering an area closed to the general public. We gazed upon sweat-lodge frames, fire rings, and a rock altar of some sort.

"This is where Crazy Horse received his name," our guide said, standing beside the rock altar. "He gained a lot of strength from this place, and the Sioux believe that, when he was forced from here, he lost spiritual strength. He died soon afterward."

Nearby was a large circle of rocks, larger than a fire ring. "They say Sweet Medicine's lodge was here," the ranger went on. "Over here," he said, pointing to a sweat lodge, "is where the Sioux medicine man Frank Fools Crow had his vision. He said he rose in a cloud and went right over there"—the ranger pointed to a cliff—"and went into the opening in the rock. There, he said he talked with God."

The ranger pointed to a tree. "At one time, this whole tree was covered with tobacco pouches and prayer flags. Now, the wind and rain have rotted most of them, and so we start all over."

He paused, gazing upon the many sweat-lodge frames. He had let it slip out—"we." In his position as ranger, he straddled both worlds. Privately, he joined traditional native people in worshipping at the mountain. Clearly, it was part of his heart and soul.

"Sweet Medicine said that the ways would die one day,"

he continued. "He predicted the alcohol and our modern way of life. He said we would lose the traditional Indian customs, but I don't think we will see that happen in our lifetime. I've seen a revival of sorts in the number of people coming here.

"I recently led a group receiving Indian religious training to this ceremonial site, but one of their requirements was to go to the cave area. Nearly all the cavern was dynamited years ago. The National Guard thought it was unsafe. Most of the nearby townspeople didn't know this is a sacred mountain. The Indians kept that secret pretty well, since the government was trying to discourage the use of Native American shrines in trying to convert the 'pagans' to Christianity. An anthropology paper brought out the mountain's true significance. Archaeologists found signs that the Cheyenne have been using this place for two thousand years, even before they lived on the plains, but it may go back three to four thousand years.

"Anyway, you can still go into the cave a ways and sit. When the group I was leading entered, I smelled something burning, like grass. Later, I was talking to a medicine man. I didn't mention the incident, but he said that if you go into the cave, sometimes you could smell the ancestors burning sweet grass. It made me feel good to know I was in tune. The cave is about a three-hour walk. Next time you come, I'll take you there.

"I try to go up the mountain every chance I get. Some people merely come to climb, but if you really focus, there's much more. I rarely go to the top. I just find the right spot and pray and meditate. I think it's good that the average tourist can come here and get a taste of what this place means. It benefits them somehow. It's tricky sometimes to balance the uses, but I believe it's working so far, and the Cheyenne are buying up land around here to prevent development and to establish a buffalo herd.

"The state bought this area in the 1960s. It has always been open to religious use by the Native Americans, and they have special access rights. This is an active cultural park, not one just to preserve unique geological strata or fauna or vegetation. Those things are important, but it is the spiritual aspects and the feeling here that matter the most. There is no question that God is here."

The ranger gazed glowingly at the hillsides and turned to us with the same warmth, "I'm glad you came!"

Chapter 7

PREPARATION

Point Reyes was a holy place where early Indians came to be healed," said Will Fudeman, our walk send-off organizer. "They believed that if you stayed too long, though, you'd go crazy. That's what happened to some of us!"

Point Reyes, California, had jumped out from the map as being a good spot for starting the walk. On our previous year's scouting mission, Steve and I hadn't made it past Utah's Zion National Park. Now, in completing last-minute scouting before the walk's first step, I was enthralled with the smooth green hills, towering redwoods, and crashing waves at Point Reyes. It was the perfect place to begin.

Traveling south for another preparatory pilgrimage of sorts, I entered an enclosure of brick, stone, and barbed wire to meet roughly thirty Native American inmates of Lompoc Federal Penitentiary. Having read about the walk in a Native American newsletter, the inmates planned to run an eighteen-mile-a-day relay for the walk's entire seven-month duration, mirroring our average daily mileage. A muscular, tattooed inmate named Ted had organized the event. He served as a spiritual guide for the group. Ironically, given the setting, Ted's clear, penetrating black eyes and welcoming smile and handshake exemplified a person who had found inner peace and freedom.

Feeling honored, I joined the inmates in a traditional sweat-lodge ceremony—a recently won freedom for them. Prison officials allowed me to bring my pipe. Ted reverently placed it on the earth altar before the blanket-covered lodge. Beneath looming gun towers and under the prison chaplain's watchful eye, I crouched on all fours and crawled into the round dome behind a line of brown bodies. We sat in a tight circle as crimson rocks were shoveled in from a nearby fire and deposited into a center pit. The door flap was closed; all was dark except for the glowing eyes before us. Water was poured on the "rock people." The leaping steam felt as though it would take my skin with it.

"Sometimes, we need to suffer ourselves," said the soft-spoken sweat leader, "to help those suffering on the outside. We come in here to let the Grandfather take all of our prejudice and animosity toward anyone. You may be praying in here and someone may come to pray next to you and you don't know if he's white, black, red, or yellow. It doesn't matter."

We each took turns praying aloud as our bodies cried and our spirits found freedom. When the sweat ended, we rinsed with a hose, only to reenter the lodge. One man explained that the inmates were allowed to sweat just twice a month for a maximum of two hours each time; every minute was precious.

For this second sweat, all rocks that remained in the fire were heaped inside, sixty-four in all. Breathing through a handful of sage helped to filter the scorching steam. With faces kept low, we sang an Indian freedom song. Humble prayers were spoken, accompanied by tears. During the last round, the inmates lit my pipe and passed it around. When the tobacco was spent, we crawled out of darkness and into light, steam rising off our bodies. We rolled onto the grass in time to see a hawk circle the gun tower. Ted leaned over to me. His dark eyes glowed. "I saw the spirit of your pipe in there," he said. "It is strong."

Before I left, the brothers ran a lap on the track with two beaded and feathered staffs, each about a foot-and-a-half long. Then they presented me with one of them for the walk. Ted explained that the staff's designs, ribbons, and tobacco ties represented the world's races and the major elements—earth, air, water, and fire—on which we all depend. "The staff is sacred," he said, "like the pipe. It was made with prayer and blessed by a medicine person. The lead walker should always hold the staff and clear the way for those who follow."

According to Ted, the staff would spiritually connect those of us on the walk with the brothers in prison, who would run with another staff on our behalf. I felt humbled by their unselfish service for people they had never met.

When I presented the sacred staff to other walkers at our preliminary meeting near Point Reyes, they were equally touched. It helped to ease anxiety. More than twenty people wished to walk the entire distance, and twice that many planned to start with us. We held long meetings to talk about our feelings, iron out logistics, and refine the walk's purpose.

While the walk promised to be a profound experience for each walker, we also felt it was important to arrange for local gatherings with communities and groups along our route and to contact local media outlets—television, newspaper, and radio—to explain our peaceful intent and purpose.

I worried about some of the walkers. Joe Schetter, for instance, a young man from St. Mary's, Ohio, was thin and pale looking. In a shy, soft-spoken manner, he expressed a desire to walk every step of the 3,800-mile journey. Given the ambitious schedule, I assumed most walkers would ride at least part of the way in our support vehicles or "sag wagons." My itinerary called for only a handful of rest days and counted on people to take turns driving ahead to arrange camp spots, media coverage, and community gatherings. Despite Joe's intent, I doubted he would last a week.

Then, too, some in our group had done very little camping, and here we were, about to camp out over two hundred nights! One person was a Floridian who had never even *seen* snow, and now we were worried about Sierra mountain passes being closed due to excess snowfall.

I also worried about how the group would mesh together. We had an ex-Green Beret/Hells Angel biker who was seeking to control his "inner dragons" and become a "warrior" of light and peace. One woman had been a nun for seven years. One man worked for Bill Graham, the rock music promoter. Another was a retired engineer who was rediscovering life as a nomad, driving a station wagon that pulled a pop-up trailer, a mobile unit he planned to bring on the walk.

One gray-bearded man, who jokingly referred to himself as "Swami Hoohaw Mugga Mugga," looked upon the walk as more of a "spiritual psychological project." Among the others were a quiet New England farmer, some ardent peace activists, and a man who was in trouble with the Internal Revenue Service for refusing to pay taxes on moral grounds.

Also with us was my wife Julie, to whom I had been married for just five months. An advocate for young children, Julie was a wonderful person. We were already having serious differences, though, which the stresses created by the walk would prove to exacerbate.

Food was another challenge. Our group included diehard vegetarians, carnivores, and junk-food addicts. One diabetic young man ate sweets to "balance out" his insulin shots. At this stage, we decided to split into food groups based upon personal preferences. Did early tribal people or settlers have to deal with such issues?

In our group were Christians, Jews, atheists, those who followed East Indian teachings, and many who upheld some form of Native American or earth-based philosophy. Some people wanted strict consensus decision making, others were satisfied with "majority rule." A small minority preferred that I fill the role of benevolent dictator. In the end, the group adopted consensus decision making with a three-fourths majority fallback vote in situations where consensus could not be reached. If three-fourths of the group could not agree on something, then we would consider the issue too divisive and drop it.

Regarding my role, I would continue to serve as walk coordinator in charge of our route, the timetable, and official correspondence. I had already determined key components or set them in motion. People were planning to join us along the route, and my position would provide continuity and help prevent the group from impulsively veering in another direction. Otherwise, I wanted minimal leadership in order to allow everyone else opportunities to facilitate meetings, speak with the media, determine camping spots, and decide a myriad of other matters. For the walk to succeed, every participant had to feel empowered.

A year and a half earlier, I had learned a valuable lesson in group empowerment. I had organized two all-night Native American Church meetings with Bear Heart in a beautiful rural setting outside Tallahassee. Three Navajo men had driven in from New Mexico, while Bear Heart and a female helper had flown in from Albuquerque and Texas, respectively. The ceremonies were deeply moving, both for the participants and for me, and everything flowed smoothly during them. But before and after them, things hadn't been as smooth. The friend sent to pick up Bear Heart and his helper at the airport had gotten lost. When they had finally arrived, Bear Heart's woman helper scolded me about the poor directions I had provided. It was a rocky start.

In between the two all-night meetings, my meal coordination was haphazard. Several women, not wanting to fall into traditional roles, had made it clear they would not do any cooking. So I had taken the cooking upon myself, yearning for some tribal sense of community where people knew how to work together.

Trying both to cook and to coordinate events made for an erratic meal schedule. I had not been a good host. To top it off, several unexpected expenses had to be paid for with my father's credit card, since the nominal donation from participants didn't come close to covering the debt. I had made the shortfall known to people, but no one offered to pitch in. A bargain was a bargain. It would take months for me to pay off the debt.

Bear Heart had picked up on my growing anxiety. The day before he was to leave, I received images of being pushed out of the nest. Was it time to fly on my own? When I drove Bear Heart to the airport for his return flight, his cold silence answered my question. My heart sank. I couldn't think of anything to say. It had happened so quickly.

Letting go: my hardest lesson. Except in dreams, that was the last time I would see Bear Heart for many years.

That whole experience could have been different had I organized a cohesive team of people to work with—people who shared in the commitment and who felt empowered in the organizational process. Had the episode occurred differently, however, perhaps I would have been less receptive to my current vision of the walk. Perhaps most of my energies would have been spent trying to organize more spiritual gatherings in Tallahassee. In any case, logic counseled that it was time to move on, but the heart doesn't always know logic.

As I looked over the assembled group at our pre-walk meeting, it was apparent that we had the stimulating elements of either a diverse, yet cohesive group, or one that might be fraught with constant turmoil. This would be my family for the next seven months. The many categories into which I had placed people, such as "farmer" or "ex-nun," would fade in time, and I would come to know each person for who they truly were. After all, these were the people in my vision of more than a year before. My true role in putting this group together was as an instrument for a Higher Power.

Some people described how—when they picked up a flyer about the walk or read about it in a magazine—something lit up inside; they simply knew they were going. "Those flyers had hooks in them," said Rosie White, the ex-nun. We had all been drawn together for a reason.

As part of our preparation, in late March 1984, a group of us traveled to San Francisco to meet with elder women from the Big Mountain area of the Navajo/Hopi Joint Use Area in Arizona. The Big Mountain area is believed to contain the largest self-sufficient native community in the lower forty-eight states. The government, responding to Hopi complaints that too many Navajo were living in the area, had begun relocating Navaho families to outlying towns. Many Navajo, bitter from having to leave their homes, suspected that mining the rich coal and uranium reserves in the area was the government's true motive.

"To move from our sacred land, our sacred peaks," said one Navaho woman tearfully, "is to die." Relocatees were having difficulty adjusting. Being rural livestock keepers, they were unaccustomed to dealing with landlords and other aspects of urban life in border towns and cities such as Flagstaff. They claimed that the government had not kept their promise to assist relocatees in their transition. Many felt swindled. They maintained that their quarrel was not with the Hopi, but with the federal government.

In response to these felt injustices, the Navajo who remained at Big Mountain had begun removing newly erected government fences, pulling up survey stakes, maintaining over-allotments of sheep, and appealing to public officials, citizens' groups, the media, and the courts.

According to the Navajo women, they were ready to move beyond nonviolent means. They were willing to go to war. Already, one of the women had shot at a crew trying to fence part of the Big Mountain area in an attempt to contain Navajo sheep herders and to separate Hopi and Navajo people. Desperation coupled with rock-hard determination seemed etched on the women's weathered faces. Something old was contained in that look. I wondered if the fabric of today's Native America would be as tightly woven if tribes had resisted the onslaught of Europeans only passively for the past five centuries. Would any red nations remain?

With the Navajo elders was a man whom I shall call Raven, a full-blooded Native American activist with the American Indian Movement, or AIM. The women had sought AIM's assistance, and Raven explained that the organization would fight for Big Mountain, spilling blood if necessary. Defiance filled his voice. Would Big Mountain be another Wounded Knee? Would the 1973 occupation of Wounded Knee by AIM activists be repeated at Big Mountain? Raven's determination caused me to question my own values. Would I fight for my home? Would I fight for land and a long-held way of life?

Years earlier, Bear Heart had given me a medicine pipe. It was for praying for healing and peace. How did this ideal fit in with war, however justified it may seem?

I wondered if public involvement, now a more visible show of support than what had occurred during past Indian wars, would prevent bloodshed and resolve the conflict peacefully.

My group offered to help spread the word about the Navajos' struggle against relocation and mining and to solicit names on a petition. We also planned to walk through the area; it had been one of the spots that jumped out at me on the map.

As we were leaving the meeting, Raven insisted on leading a sweat-lodge ceremony for us the next day. Having been a part of the Native Americans' Longest Walk across the country in 1978, he felt a kinship with walkers. "On the first day," he said, "Dennis Banks took the staff and led us fifty miles until we found a place to stay. We had no advance crew or planning, and no one gave us a sweat beforehand. I want you guys to have a better start."

The next day, Raven was true to his promise—he gathered us at his sweat lodge high on a cliff overlooking the Pacific Ocean. It was a sun-dance sweat lodge, he said; the door faced west. Raven's purple chest scars testified to participation in eight Lakota sun-dance ceremonies.

Outside the lodge around the fire, with his long black hair pushed back, Raven bellowed orders to his blonde-haired fire tender. "More wood on this side. You can't have a sweat unless the rocks are really hot!" Once in the lodge, however, with door flaps closed and steam leaping, Raven became a calm channel for spiritual guidance. "Eagles will watch over you," he said. "Many peyote meetings and sun dances will pray for you. The four-leggeds, two-leggeds, and winged ones will be watching you. I will come to check on you as the raven. Each morning, offer tobacco and state your purpose. The medicine people will support you. . . ."

Then Raven said something I especially noted in regard to Joe, the sickly looking man who wanted to walk every step of the journey: "The weakest among you shall be the strongest."

During breaks, when the door was opened and water passed, Raven revealed a keen love for banter. He asked fifty-six-year-old Ralph Cobb from where he originated.

"Oklahoma," Ralph replied.

"Oh, so you're a redneck."

"No."

"But the only people in Oklahoma are Indians and rednecks."

"Well, then, I'm a sympathetic redneck." Many in the lodge chuckled, including Raven.

Everything about the sweat was challenging—the cramped lodge and heat and the steep, rocky descent to water afterward, through poison oak, no less! As everything in the native way was symbolic of something, I wondered if these difficult conditions might suggest the nature of the months to come.

The sweats took longer than expected, and we pulled into the Point Reyes Youth Hostel later than planned. Raven was driving his own pickup truck. The curator greeted us at the entrance. Good naturedly, he guided our vehicles to a parking area. For some reason, Raven was not complying.

"Sir, would you please park in the parking area," the curator asked a second time, more firmly. Raven turned off his engine and burst open the door.

"Are you giving me a hassle?" he yelled, stalking to within inches of the man's startled face. Instinctively, I stepped between them to prevent violence. Raven had begun cursing him. The curator asked Raven to leave, and

Raven agreed. Having seen no provocation for his attack, I did not argue. Then Raven turned on me!

"You've got a lot to learn about us American Indian Movement people," he said. "You don't brush us off. We always stick up for each other no matter what. We've been stepped on for too long."

"We've agreed to a nonviolence code, Raven," I said. "We will not initiate any violence, and I saw no reason for you to start a fight with that man."

"I just picked up on something, that's all. You know, I was wondering about you people. You're going to have trouble from us. I'm going to get my AIM brothers all over the country to get you people and rip that pipe from you, Doug. I was wondering about you and that pipe."

"What's gotten into you, Raven? There's no reason for all of this." My blood was pumping faster.

Raven inched closer to my face. "What would you do right now if I hit you?"

"If you push me far enough, I'll have to defend myself," I said. "Otherwise, I will not fight you."

Almost instinctively, I sat on the ground, making myself more vulnerable in the hope he would not see a challenge. I tried to focus on love and peace, but part of me wanted to belt Raven for being such a jerk. Realizing that some of my thoughts were becoming violent, I tried to clear them, asking for spiritual help. Raven glared at me. My adrenaline was flowing.

"Come on, Raven," I said, finally, standing up. "Let's go in and have some dinner." I extended the invitation a second time.

"Okay, let's go." He seemed to lighten up a degree.

We walked inside the dormitory where the group had cooked and set food out. They had heard the yelling, and the room quieted when we entered. Looking at their worried faces, I had a sudden thought: Change the walk route and make a beeline to Washington, D.C., skipping all Native American reservations. The walk was dangerous, I now realized. A pall had been cast over it. Instead of establishing a bridge of friendship with native people, our group would resemble pioneers in a wagon train on the lookout for hostile ambushes. Bearing in mind the Wounded Knee occupation and other incidents, I knew the American Indian Movement wasn't a group to mess around with. And we would be on their turf.

Raven broke the silence with his deep, booming voice. "In our culture, we clear the air of our emotions before we eat. Something happened outside that caused me to question your group's nonviolence code. I want to hear what this nonviolence code means to you." Now Raven was challenging the whole group. Admittedly, he had guts.

After a silence, a few in our group started to answer. We were still new to each other and I was curious about the question myself.

"If we are to spread peace," said one walker, "we must be nonviolent. We have to practice what we preach." Several others versed similar sentiments. Raven took a deep breath, looking at everyone accusingly.

"You people have a choice to be nonviolent," he began, scowling. "Most of you are white and middle class. Many of us have had no choice. We've been beaten, thrown in jail for no reason, and discriminated against. Finally, we said, 'Enough, we've got to fight back!' The American Indian

Movement was born. Sometimes we have to initiate violence to prevent further violence upon us. But most of the time, we are simply defending ourselves and our Mother Earth. Many people say, 'Why are you so violent? Oh, AIM is so violent.' But they don't understand where we've come from. Still, most of what we do is nonviolent. Violence is the last resort."

Raven then asked me to respond. I stood and tried to measure my words carefully. Everyone remained tense and quiet. "In many ways, we do have more of a choice because of our background," I began, "but as far as promoting positive change, AIM must appeal to people's hearts with love, not violence. We must all do that. I empathize with you, Raven, and, yes, in some cases I would defend myself and others. But I would not initiate violence or try to provoke it. If I defended myself from an attack, I would hope my defense would stop if the attack stopped." Many others agreed, pointing out to Raven that we could promote the same goals of AIM through peaceful means.

"Maybe then," Raven said firmly, "you should call your code a peace code, not a nonviolence code, as most of you would defend yourselves with violent means if necessary." He paused and looked at me. "If at any point any AIM member gives you trouble on the walk or with your pipe, Doug, tell them I said you were alright." The air seemed clear. Raven said a blessing for our now cold meal.

During dinner, a walker approached me. "I just heard Raven talking. He said you passed some sort of test outside. You stuck by your principles. I also heard him say you were the first white pipe carrier he had met who didn't get his pipe ripped away."

In the Plains tradition, a medicine pipe is earned by an individual and is presented by a recognized spiritual leader. It is considered an honor and a responsibility not to be taken lightly. With a medicine pipe, you smoke and pray for clarity and for the healing of others. People in need might gift you with tobacco and ask that you smoke for them. In more modern times, controversy has arisen over pipes that have been bought and sold or which have been presented by persons whose tribal affiliations or status has been questioned by some. The possession of medicine pipes by non-Indians or by persons with a small amount of Indian ancestry has also been controversial, especially among many AIM activists.

And, needless to say, to Raven and those like him, I was a non-Indian. Any remote Indian ancestry I might have had didn't count. Under the circumstances, I was simply glad Raven respected Bear Heart and maybe me enough to leave my pipe alone. Still, I wondered, was the whole walk going to be as fraught with trouble?

Chapter

8

THE WALK FOR THE EARTH

Raven was in good spirits in the morning. He told me the walk should be kept peaceful, and he apologized to the hostel curator for the previous evening's episode, giving him a white feather. Whether he had planned the incident as a test or not, it had clarified our values as a group before we actually took the first step. It had also given us a better understanding of the pain and frustration many native people experience.

Under huge redwoods at the Bear Valley picnic ground at Point Reyes, more than a hundred people assembled for our send-off. Ironically, it was April 1, April Fools Day. We made a huge circle, and anyone could share a message, prayer, or song. Many expressed how they felt upon having left jobs, possessions, security, and loved ones to walk seven months across the country for principles in which they believed. It was the first such total lifestyle change for many. Our excitement was mixed with anxiety. Three seasons would pass before we reached Washington, D.C. What would our group be like then?

Ten-year-old Michael Perdue of Harbin Hot Springs, California, planned to walk to the Four Corners, which would take almost two months. He recited a moving poem he had written:

> We have lost the secret of the tribe:
> The tribe of the good, the tribe of knowledge that
>   holds our minds.
> It seeks the wind;
> It's like an owl that glides in the sky.
> It knows the truth and the truth only.
> What could it be, this thing that runs through us
>   every once in awhile
> Like a flash of lightning?
> It searches the night that no longer holds the truth
> Of knowledge, strength, ability, wisdom, and courage.
> Only a few have these treasures
> And those are the ones left of the tribe.

Our sixty-six-year-old elder, Alice Massie of West Virginia, nodded her approval. She planned to walk with us for most of the journey. Our youngest participant, six-month-old Psalm, fidgeted in her mother's arms. The walk group was taking on an extended-family feeling.

Raven was the last to speak in the circle. "You are walking for the Indian because you are walking for the land," he said. "You are fulfilling Indian prophecy that speaks of white people walking for the earth. The red people and the yellow people [the Buddhists] have already walked across the land. When the black people walk, then we shall all walk together. This walk is more important than most people think."

Raven fanned the walkers with cedar smoke and a huge eagle wing. Then everyone lined up, facing east. Together, across lush, green grass, we took the first of what would be several million steps. Part of a vision was being fulfilled. I felt the prayers of many people who had helped us reach this successful beginning.

Young Michael best summed up the day in his journal: "First day was easy. An Indian gave us an eagle feather ceremony. Then we took the first step together. I was beating the drum. We only did three miles. It was great."

I wondered how months of walking across the land with this newly formed tribe would shape the kind of person Michael would become. What example would he set for other children? What would he teach us?

Two days later, on our first full day of walking—seventeen miles—my preliminary tensions faded as my blisters grew. Ron Greenlight, our herbalist, provided nibbles and remedies from roadside finds: wild broccoli, onions, stinging nettle, cattails, watercress. . . . He planned to spend little money on food and was eager to share the philosophy behind his practice. "When I pick a fruit or plants, I make sure I plant some seeds," he explained, reflecting guidance he had received from a Cherokee medicine man. "It's important to give back to the earth when taking from her."

Raven returned a few days later to walk and offer guidance. "I kept sending ravens to check on you and they never came back," he joked. "So I thought I'd better come myself." We had, in fact, seen a profusion of ravens.

Around a campfire along the Sacramento River, Raven filled a large, red stone pipe with pure tobacco for all to smoke. Our campfire accentuated his dark brown skin and jet-black long hair. With his chunky, heavy-boned features and booming voice, he could be intimidating. At other times, he showed a little boy smile, humor, and sincerity. Was his dichotomy of traits preparing us for walking through the reservations?

"Many Indians will be watching you for the example that you set," Raven began, putting the filled pipe down and lighting cedar needles in an abalone shell. "Many of you may not want to be Indian, but you will be because you have suffered during the long days of walking; you are suffering for everyone." With an eagle wing, he fanned the smoldering cedar as he spoke, pausing periodically.

"I feel you shall go to a sun dance in South Dakota . . . and I will dance a whole day for you at the next sun dance at Big Mountain. I hope the Indian will receive you well. I feel you shall be adopted into some tribes. You shall also talk to the Hopi brothers. The peyote will look at you in the Four Corners.

"The Southwest Indian people may react very quietly to you at first, but, believe me, they will be watching you. How you treat the staff is important. You will be very strong by the time you hit the Southwest, and medicine people will pick up on that. A true medicine person is colorblind.

"I am not a medicine man, but I know of these ways; I have been through eight sun dances. My way is the sun-dance way. Doug, you need to go to a sun dance and bring your pipe. These things speak to me—the cedar, the fire, the pipe. You need to respect all life, even the animals you find dead along the road. . . . Soon, you will be a rainbow group. Many more will join you."

He waved cedar smoke over the pipe and lit the tobacco with a burning stick from the fire. He began passing it around the circle in a clockwise motion. The pipe went out a little over halfway around. "You need to work on unifying as a group!" he growled. "This pipe has stayed lit for fifty people at Big Mountain. Where the pipe stopped, you need to work on that!"

In the pipe circle, many people voiced prayers and concerns. Raven asked me to speak. I relayed how the animals, by acting as spiritual messengers, could tell us when one of our group needed help, how the Creator could help us all to think with one mind so we would not, as Raven put it, walk in twenty-five different directions. I thanked Raven for helping me realize how a greater sharing with Indian people could occur.

Afterward, we drummed and sang around the fire. Many songs were English adaptations of native songs, or they were new songs that reflected a native philosophy. Raven just nodded and listened, with the drumbeats echoing across the valley.

He stayed with us longer than he had expected. His last night was at Indian Grinding Rock State Park, ancestral home of the Miwok. No Miwok Indians were present, but a large, round, cedar ceremonial house at the park served as their gathering place. Their ancestors had left hundreds of holes in granite, once used for pounding acorns into flour.

For Miwok culture to have survived the tumultuous 1800s is considered miraculous. Gold seekers and lumbermen disrupted their peaceful existence. The state's first gold strike occurred only miles away. Mine shafts pierced the earth, hills were stripped of trees, and streams became clogged with silt and logs. Miwoks and other native people were forced to work for the very exploiters who were destroying their land and lifestyle, if they weren't displaced or killed outright.

Today, trees again blanket the hills. Streams run clear in upper altitudes. And refuges such as Indian Grinding Rock State Park harbor centuries-old oak trees and remnants of an ancient way of life.

We were on our way. The walk had begun, and the California spring caressed us with sunshine, warm breezes, and sweet aromas. We walked east in an easy, uplifting manner, across land still sacred to native people. But the Sierra Mountains lay before us, snow covered and formidable looking. They would be our first physical obstacle.

Chapter
9

PASSAGE

The weather in the Sierra Mountains was cold and crystal clear—we were blessed. Roadsides and mountains were deep in snow. Lakes lay frozen and white. Yet the mountain passes were open for the first time since the previous year.

From a lofty 8,650 feet, Carson Pass presented us with an unforgettable wintry vista. Once when we were sprawled across sun-warmed rocks along the pass, pleasantly tired, a sudden image caught our attention. Against a clear sky, a huge bird flew overhead. The silhouette was unmistakable—an eagle—one that was solid white. A V-shaped flock of snow geese followed. Could it mean something?

We safely crossed Monitor Pass two days later and descended through a deeply etched valley, one where boulders and cliffs seemed to speak their history. The walk was a mere flash in time—a streak of sunlight—when compared to these ancient witnesses, but I wanted to live it fully and richly, honoring those who had also walked this way. Perhaps the earth remembers her pilgrims.

We camped beside a rushing stream under huge ponderosa pines. Four Jewish walkers cooked a Passover Seder dinner for the entire group. It seemed appropriate, given our safe passage over the wintry Sierra range. When the sun had set and we were sitting upon pine needles around a fire, Leslie (who had changed her last name from Good*man* to Good*woman* because she was a "good woman") welcomed us for the dinner.

"As we were preparing the meal," she began, "we felt closer to our roots. We who cooked the meal have been raised Jewish, but we have not practiced our faith for a long time. There was something about cooking on the ground in the wilds that touched us. The Jews were a very earth-loving, tribal people. Preparing for this meal was different from the usual week-long modern preparation with ovens, blenders, fine china, and fancy goblets. It helped us feel in tune with the earth."

Leslie went on to tell the story of Moses and the flight from Egypt and to describe other aspects of Passover. Then she explained how the Egyptians were punished with ten plagues for not allowing the Jews to leave Egypt. Most of the plagues related to human health and the environment, including a river being turned to blood; frogs overrunning Egypt; infestations of fleas, flies, and locusts; epidemic livestock diseases; skin boils; fiery hail; three days of utter darkness; and the death of Egyptian first-born males.

Historical detectives and scientists have theorized that some of the plagues could be explained by volcanic activity or by toxic red algae caused by pollution that set off a chain of ecological catastrophes.

"Those times were similar to these in that purification was necessary," Leslie continued. "Mother Earth may respond to the abuse she has received in the form of earthquakes, volcanoes, and the like."

The idea of earth changes did not seem foreign to us as we sat on the ground, our bodies aglow in moonlight as subfreezing temperatures crept in. In the past week, we had had to worry about avalanches, blizzards, extreme cold, and snow-blocked mountain passes, so our respect for the elements had become greatly enhanced. Many of us had grown stronger, and we celebrated with traditional Jewish songs and dances. More wood was added to the fire, casting a brighter light on the festivities. Rosie, the former nun, summarized the mood: "It's about time the Jews and Catholics got together!"

Ringed by ancient volcanoes, Mono Lake sat like a huge silver-blue saucer twice the size of San Francisco. Mark Twain had labeled the lake a "lifeless sea," yet millions of birds flock to it annually to feed on trillions of brine shrimp. The unusual, jutting, tufa rock formations attract hordes of tourists.

We hiked along Mono Lake to the town of Lee Vining, home of the Save the Mono Lake Committee Center, our host for the weekend. The lake was fed by several freshwater streams that the City of Los Angeles had been diverting for its own use for decades. The committee's goal was to prevent the city from increasing these diversions—the fear being that the consequential rise in the lake's salinity would disrupt the food chain. Moreover, since diversions had begun in 1941, the level of the lake had been dropping steadily, further upsetting its equilibrium. The Mono Lake Committee appealed to the courts, but, as one activist put it: "Ultimately, the lake has to be saved through the hearts of the people, who must become willing to take some simple steps to conserve water. That's partly what you walkers are accomplishing—appealing to people's hearts." Besides communicating with people we met, we would distribute brochures that explained the issue, and we planned to talk with the media.

The activist added that nearby volcanoes might do the job for them by melting the Los Angeles pipeline. We hoped it wouldn't come to that. Besides, if people on the other end of the pipeline didn't voluntarily change water-consumption habits, the pipeline would simply be rebuilt.

As a footnote, I should add that, several years after the walk, and primarily due to the Mono Lake Committee's unceasing efforts, a court order mandated that the City of Los Angeles reduce the diversion of water from streams leading into the lake. As a result, lake levels have risen ten feet, helping to ensure the lake's delicate ecological balance. The court ruling forced the city to promote serious water conservation and recycling. Los Angeles now uses water at 1970s levels, even though its population has risen by a third. The precedent-setting case could help efforts to protect other wild places around the country.

The Mono Lake Committee is now focusing on restoring streams and wetlands of the Mono Basin. Its efforts are helping Los Angeles and other cities meet their water needs without transferring environmental problems to other areas.

Eagle Man, a Paiute medicine man, had been in the midst of the Los Angeles-related water wars. On the walk, we visited him at his modest home near Bishop, California, for a sweat-lodge ceremony. "A long time ago, they tried to move all the Indians and white people from this land so they could flood this whole valley for a reservoir," he said. "But we wouldn't go. This is our home. We could have destroyed their plans using our medicine ways, but a lot of innocent people would have suffered as a result. That is not my way. I made a vow to help anyone who comes to me, whether they are white, red, black, or yellow."

After entering Eagle Man's huge sweat lodge, we sat on woven tule mats as red-hot volcanic rocks were brought in by pitchfork and placed in a center pit. Then the door was closed—enveloping us in darkness. We each prayed in our own way. Songs and chants were shared. Flaps were opened and Eagle Man asked us to bless ourselves, whereupon we lightly slapped hands over our bodies, infusing our pores with positive energy. Then more hot rocks were brought in. After three more of these cycles, flaps were opened for the last time and a medicine pipe was passed. We then rinsed ourselves with a hose and sat down for a feast in a long, windowless building.

With a jovial, half-toothless smile, Eagle Man cracked jokes, occasionally interjecting profound advice and wisdom. "Don't believe anything I say," said the stocky elder, smiling, "I'm just an old bullshitter." (That was the only line of his I didn't believe.) "This walk you are doing is a good thing," he continued. "Even the people who oppose you at first will benefit. Every morning when you give your prayer for the walk, wherever you are, often a medicine person will see you doing it. He will be able to tell that your intentions are good." I gathered from Eagle Man that the walk's greatest impact would be on a spiritual level, from prayers and from one-on-one communication.

Eagle Man asked me to say the meal blessing. Afterward, he said, half-seriously: "What are you, some kind of medicine man?"

"I'm a pipe carrier," I replied shyly.

"You don't have to tell a medicine person you are a pipe carrier—they'll know. And they'll help you in their own way. You have a lot to learn about that pipe. I could have sent Buffalo Calf Woman to you in the sweat to teach you a lot more real quick."

White Buffalo Calf Woman was a mythic figure of Lakota Indian legend who first brought the pipe to the people. At one point, she met a man with impure thoughts and turned him into a pile of bones. White Buffalo Calf Woman didn't mess around. How serious was Eagle Man?

Eagle Man puffed on a cigarette and chuckled. "The spirits tell me it's easier to learn lessons here than in the spirit world." He shrugged and rolled another cigarette with his cracked, brown hands. "Anyway, that's what they tell me." Was he an old bullshitter? A lightness about him told me I was with an enlightened being—he wasn't perfect, but then who was?

Dusty dogs scurried about Eagle Man's dilapidated trailer as we left. His last words to me were, "As you walk, keep looking up, up." His helper from the sweat said that Eagle Man's spirit flies as the white eagle. Did he have some connection to the mysterious bird we had seen over Carson Pass?

Many cultures have huge stone cathedrals, temples, or ashrams where their priests and spiritual teachers lead others in worship. Eagle Man's place of worship was a simple sweat lodge; his kingdom was the sky.

In the days that followed, instead of looking up, I often looked down upon the Nevada desert scrub. Fascinating rocks drew my attention. Many seemed to reflect the horror that occurred beneath the surface. We skirted just north and east of the Nevada Test Site. Some of the rocks were filled with exploding red and orange hues; and, if that wasn't symbolic enough, Rosie found a mushroom-shaped rock.

Late one day, a government man drove up and calmly informed us that an underground nuclear test would occur the next morning. "Don't be alarmed by a booming sound," he said. Then he drove away.

"Don't be alarmed": That's the same message the government had given to nearby communities between 1951 and 1962, when more than a hundred atomic bombs were detonated above ground at the test range, twenty-three being larger than the one dropped on Hiroshima. Herds of livestock had perished, and thousands of people were subsequently ravaged by cancers and other illnesses.

A wide range of emotions swept through our group—fear, concern, helplessness. Understandably, Leslie and her baby left. "It feels like a disease under the skin of the earth," said Susie, at age eighteen the youngest adult with us. Since the overall group feeling was that the walk was a positive healing journey rather than a protest march, many people chose to build a large medicine wheel in the desert. A string of rocks was laid in each of the four directions to make a natural cross. Finished off with an outer and an inner circle of stones, one at the circumference and one near the center, it was similar to medicine wheels that are hundreds and thousands of years old and that still exist in North America—ancient altars of the earth. The most famous is Wyoming's Bighorn Medicine Wheel, but many more medicine wheels have been documented, mostly in the northern plains. They are places for prayer and meditation.

We lit a fire in the wheel's center. Each person shared his or her feelings. The land, we felt, needed love, not fear. Love was more powerful. We sang songs of celebration and healing. We felt confident that we would pass through the bomb test unscathed. And we hoped that, as public awareness heightened about the long-term effects of nuclear tests, they would one day be rendered obsolete.

It would be eight more years before nuclear-bomb testing at the Nevada Test Site would cease in 1992. Then, in 2005, discussion arose about restarting the program in light of plans for a new class of "bunker busting" nuclear warheads. In fact, funding for producing nuclear weapons rose to more than six billion dollars in 2006. This in turn has been helping to raise the demand for uranium mining and exacerbating the problems associated with nuclear waste disposal.

At the request of Western Shoshone spiritual leader Corbin Harney, the Shundahai Network was formed in 1994 by a council of long-term nuclear disarmament activists. *Shundahai* is a Western Shoshone word for "peace and harmony with all creation." The network's goal is to break the nuclear chain of mining, transportation, use, and waste disposal and to push for complete nuclear disarmament.

Over the years, Shundahai has evolved into an international network of activists and organizations, helping to bridge the gap between indigenous communities and groups and individuals working on environmental, peace, and justice issues. They are pushing to close the Nevada Test Site and to halt high-level nuclear waste dumps at Nevada's Yucca Mountain and the Skull Valley Reservation.

No booms were felt the next morning, but a government man dropped by in the afternoon and told us the blast had occurred around noon. Government officials never hindered our passage, but their frequent surveillance was apparent. Helicopters and fighter jets often flew close to us. One helicopter hovered an alarming fifty feet above our heads while we still lay in sleeping bags under a cloudless morning sky. For the most part, however, we enjoyed the immense unspoiled valleys tinted with pastel shades of red, purple, brown, and green. Early travelers would have witnessed scenes little different from the ones we saw.

Our appreciation of the land's wildness wasn't shared by everyone we met. "Why, I wouldn't even get out of my car after Coyote Summit," exclaimed a waitress in Rachel, Nevada—population eighty. "So many poisonous sidewinders are coming out of hibernation in that next valley. And I sure wouldn't sleep there!" It was another scare story to go along with ones about deadly blizzards, avalanches, blistering heat, mauling mountain lions, and hostile "rednecks" or Indians. We did vow to be wary of rattlesnakes, though, as temperatures were rising every day.

The warnings reminded me of Florida tales about bloodthirsty alligators, snakes, and sharks. Every area has such stories. The land should be respected, but not feared. It was fear and lack of appreciation that perpetuated a commonly held belief that the rugged Nevada landscape was a wasteland and hence appropriate as a national sacrifice area for nuclear-bomb tests, waste disposal, and strip mines. It is the environmental version of dehumanizing the enemy by throwing out demeaning labels. Then why, I wondered, did this "wasteland" fill me with a feeling as large as the land itself?

My spirit ran with ever-present winds and poked into crevices and rabbit holes like a coyote. Wildflowers—intricate desert ornaments—intoxicated me with their beauty. I found rough turquoise rocks and a finely carved Shoshone stone scraper. This "wasteland" was more like salvation for a restless soul. Others in our group expressed similar feelings. Our hearts swelled with the land's powerful beauty. It helped to create a newfound cohesion.

We camped every night near the highway with few, if any, vehicles passing us after dark. We created our own entertainment—songs, stories, jokes, games—or we would hike around our camp to get a better view of the sunset and emerging stars. Sometimes, desert hikes revealed striking petroglyphs on boulders and rock walls. One depicted native people herding wild animals into a type of corral. How odd that native people were driven from this area more than a century before, only for the land to remain virtually uninhabited.

The Nevada wilds marked a time when we were better adjusting to the physical rigors of the walk. Blisters were healing. Skin color was changing from burnt red to dark brown. Even Joe—who at the outset had looked so frail and had alarmed us by vowing to walk every step—had now grown dark, bearded, and healthy looking. At one point in California, some of us had contemplated forcing Joe to refrain from walking for a period because of severe sunburn and possible sun poisoning on his arms and legs. He doggedly refused to stop or to allow us to get a closer look at his burns, but he did begin to cover his limbs and put on salve. His skin healed after a few days. He had already walked beyond the expectations of most of us.

Near Nevada's end, we received positive feedback. By calling a friend in California, a walker learned that Raven's exposure to the walk had helped him to trust other non-Indian people to a greater extent. Some of his native friends were also behaving more openly. This was the type of positive chain reaction I had hoped the walk would achieve.

Soon, we would enter Indian country, including the largest reservation in the United States—that of the Navajo Nation. I hoped that our good fortune would continue and that our message would be received in a positive way.

Chapter
10

DESERT PEOPLES

range and purple sunset hues splashed across dry mesas as we settled into our campsite on northern Arizona's Kaibab Paiute Indian Reservation. Part of the Southern Paiute Nation, these are a people who can trace their ancestry to desert cultures that thrived ten thousand years ago. They have been known as the Kaibab Paiutes for almost nine hundred years, ever since the Paiute band settled on the Kaibab Plateau—*Kaibab* being a Paiute word meaning "The Mountain Lying Down." I had sent a letter to the tribal chairperson months earlier, but she had never answered it. She merely waited for our arrival and arranged for a potluck dinner with Paiute families. It was a good time around a crackling fire.

With a shy humbleness, Paiute elder Dan Bullet relayed a story of three Paiutes who had nearly died of thirst after embarking on a long journey, even though they were steeped in survival knowledge. "Traveling wasn't easy in the old days," he concluded. At the evening's end, he pulled four crumpled dollars from his pocket and placed them in my hand as a donation for the walk. I acknowledged the gift by presenting him with a walk T-shirt.

At one time, the Paiute people were more numerous and spread out through the Southwest. Now, the band numbers around two hundred, or about thirty families. In order to avoid the pitfalls of other reservations, they have a strict no-alcohol policy, although there is no one to enforce it except the reservation's one policeman.

Before dawn the next morning, it became clear that this policy was easily violated. Three drunken Paiutes awakened me, wanting a ride up the road. I politely refused, as no one else was awake and several people were sleeping in the support vehicles. If we could walk thousands of miles, they could make it two miles without waking the entire camp, I figured. Reluctantly, the Paiutes left, complaining loudly. Indian alcoholism, a chronic problem, was the issue we had received the most warnings about.

At a reasonable hour, under bright sun, we walked the reservation's educational trails and found Indian petroglyphs. One rock drawing of an eagle man was similar to copper breastplate designs found in temple mounds near Tallahassee. Such similarities between cultures that are separated by great distances always intrigue me.

As we were walking east on Highway 389, a Native American in a dusty red sports car shocked us back to the present. He stopped at the head of our walk line, his car engine growling. "I haven't seen this many white people in years," he snarled, slurring his words. "I'm going to get some of my friends in Tuba City to come after you. You'll see!" After a heated discussion, the man quieted only when fifteen Paiute school children and their parents arrived to walk with us. His car spewed gravel as he exited.

Proudly, the young people took turns carrying the sacred staff at the head of our line. Passing drivers honked and waved. The young walkers smiled; they held their heads high. I wished they could walk with us for the remainder of our journey.

The Paiute students, who attended school with non-Indians, told us of how they were fighting segregation on school buses and of how they had refused to study a Paiute skeleton in biology class. After much protest, the tribal elders had succeeded in obtaining the skeleton and burying it, but the school-bus fight was still looming.

In the evening, the elders joined us again at a roadside camp. They took turns holding our staff. "I have not seen one of these for many years," said one elder, admiring the beadwork. "We have lost many of our ways."

With warm goodbyes, the Paiute families left just after sunset. Their exit marked the arrival of the lone reservation policeman. As he drove up, his truck lights glared into our camp. He stepped out, his massive body silhouetted by the bright beams. "Have you seen anyone unusual in the area this evening?" the officer asked gruffly.

"No, Sir," we responded.

The policeman moved closer; he clutched a long, black flashlight. "About an hour ago, a stolen U-Haul was found on fire only a few miles from here. We have no leads. You people are the only strangers in this area. That burning truck doesn't make you look good!" He paused, as if carefully choosing his next words. He seemed to be looking for any excuse to get under our skin. He was succeeding.

"I see a lot of problems for you on the Navajo Reservation because you are mostly non-Indians," he said, the edge in his voice becoming sharper. "There are many more of them than there are of you. This is just a small reservation." The officer scanned the camp with his flashlight. Abruptly, he climbed back into his truck and retreated into the desert night. He took our good mood with him.

Lying awake that night, thinking of how unaccustomed I was to being a minority, or to being so visible or vulnerable, I looked back on my vision. I had been moved to bring the walk through native lands in order to understand and support native struggles. This experience was simply another test, I told myself. It would get better. We walked the same land native people walked, suffered under the same hot sun, watched the same sunsets. We were different than camera-toting tourists seeking to buy trinkets.

I also wondered how I could be so naive in thinking that, after five hundred years of oppression, native people would simply welcome us like long-lost cousins. Why should they? Maybe they just wanted to be left alone.

Sleep did not come easily. When it did, my dreams continued to mirror my inner conflict.

Soon after dawn, we drove back to the tribal headquarters to check on the U-Haul incident. In a monotone reminiscent of Sergeant Friday on *Dragnet*, the tribal policeman informed us that the culprit had been apprehended; he wasn't a member of our group. Relieved, we shook his hand as an act of goodwill. As we moved on, it was with many positive memories of the Kaibab Paiutes, but I felt some trepidation upon entering the Navajo Reservation. The policeman's warning came back to me: "There are many more of them than there are of you."

As the days progressed, we developed a deeper respect for the hardships native people have always endured in the area. Temperatures soared to 110 degrees. One could consume water surprisingly fast and still suffer heat stroke. We risked becoming human French fries. Each walking day began before dawn so that we could retreat into shade during the hottest part of the afternoon. Only six weeks earlier, we had been trudging through Sierra snow.

As we had done in Nevada, we tried walking cross-country. We soon found that seemingly flat land was fissured with precipitous canyons. They were good places to cool off in, but crossing them was impossible.

We passed one scorching afternoon in a road culvert, making primitive music with rocks and sticks. The rhythms helped us forget the heat. Didn't Moses and his people wander the deserts for forty years? A month or so during one summer was enough for me.

Ron, our walking herbalist, showed us ways to survive on desert plants such as cactus and yucca. It was easy to imagine that his teaching only refreshed in us a knowledge that had been embedded deep in the human psyche since antiquity. It gave us more confidence in walking.

One early, pre-dawn start enabled us to trek twenty-three miles along Marble Canyon's spectacular red cliffs. We camped beside the icy Colorado River at Lee's Ferry. It was the only natural river crossing for hundreds of miles, being a place where the towering cliffs on both sides dipped low enough so that people could pass. Native peoples had used the crossing for millennia, followed by settlers. In the days when they had waded or swum across the river without a bridge, vital supplies had often been swept away by fast currents, or enemies had lurked on the other side. Sometimes, lives were lost.

That evening, under a pale moonlight, the shadowy cliffs bore silent witness to one of our walk's periodic "heart meetings," in which everyone was free to express their emotions. Tears flowed. The starkness of the desert was exposing the insecurities and fear that many of us carried in our lives.

As an added stress, the owners of two of our three support vans were scheduled to leave within days, and they would take their vehicles with them. Our group still numbered more than thirty. The one lone van that remained would not be large enough to accommodate all our gear, much less pick up tired walkers, and its owner was reluctant to double back and forth all day long since the van was showing obvious signs of wear. Our schedule called for averaging eighteen miles a day in order to finish the walk by winter, but backpacking that far daily through desert heat and the subsequent Rocky Mountains was unrealistic for many in our group. We were trying to create a supportive environment, but Mother Nature wasn't helping. Indeed, two crawling scorpions interrupted the meeting. And the roar of the Colorado's swift crashing water failed to soothe tensions.

"It's interesting that all of these problems are happening now," said Hal, an especially insightful walker. "I can better appreciate the strength of the Native Americans who learned to survive here with so little."

The next evening, after covering more than twenty hot miles, we met about our support-vehicle situation. The general state of anxiety aggravated numerous personality differences. I got into a stupid argument, partly due to my fear that the group might break apart. The fire flickered on tense faces—thirty-five diverse people fighting each other in a gravel pit, surrounded by desert and scattered hogans. The expansive land offered nowhere to hide to prevent us from facing the dragons emerging from within. We felt out of place. How did we come to this? What were we doing anyway? Would just a few strong walkers continue while all the others headed home? It felt like a Darwinian twist on the "survival of the fittest."

At some point after midnight, the energy shifted, followed by tears and hugs. A walker who needed healing sat in the middle as we circled around him and lay hands upon his head and shoulders, while some of us chanted his name. For a few brief moments, we were of one mind. Darkness evaporated. I was sure everyone had felt it. In one evening, we had experienced both the negative and the positive extremes of our group's potential.

One realistic outcome was that we agreed to pitch in and buy a used pickup truck to help haul gear. Hope was emerging. We would stay together, after all, and face the challenging months ahead as one group.

As the days progressed, we were relieved to find friendly and open Navajo people. It seemed as if everyone had heard of us prior to our arrival via the "moccasin telegraph," a term they used for news that traveled quickly by word of mouth. People invited us to camp on their land each night, some speaking only enough English to say, "You are welcome here." One small storeowner wanted to empty his shelves to give us food. We only took a small portion of his generous offer. In turn, we set up a give-away box of items for native people we met in an effort to create good will and to reduce our gear volume. The gifts were well received.

Near the Hopi Reservation, we were invited to traditional kachina dances in Moenkopi, a largely ancient Hopi village. A main purpose of the dances is to seek the aid of supernatural beings in securing favorable weather for successful harvests of crops such as corn, a Hopi mainstay. We joined a throng of Hopi who encircled a rectangular plaza. Some sat on the flat rooftops of adobe structures. People talked excitedly and laughed easily. We were within the borders of the United States of America, but this was a nation altogether different from the one we knew, a land some have labeled "the Tibet of the West."

Everyone quieted as a line of stocky men, each wearing identically sculpted kachina masks, trotted into the plaza with soldier-like precision. Low chants seemed to rumble straight from their gut. I was gripped by the moment's awesome magic.

The dancers portrayed thunder gods. In fact, at that moment, they were believed to *be* thunder gods descending upon the people, gods who brought rain and spiritual blessings. The dance served as a spiritual conduit.

Then the Hopi clowns suddenly appeared, and the kachina dancers quietly shuffled away. Stark white clay completely covered the clowns' bodies, including their loincloths, skin, hair, and even eyebrows. Their reckless skits shocked me back into mainstream Western culture. They portrayed foul-mouthed drug addicts, sex perverts, materialistic people, and corrupt politicians. No circus would dare have them, but the Hopi crowd roared their approval.

One Hopi elder beside me leaned over, kindly offering an explanation. Perhaps he had observed my shocked expression. "The clowns are meant to depict the sort of behavior a traditional Hopi should avoid," he began. "Their skits always change with the times, depending on what external influences are affecting the tribe. The kachina dances, on the other hand, pretty much remain the same, upholding the dignity of the Hopi. They evolve more slowly, like nature."

The energy shifted back and forth from the ribald clowns to the focused intent of the kachina dancers. The contrast enhanced the quality and purpose of each.

During one skit, the clowns yanked many walkers onto the plaza for a mock dance. I was one of the lucky chosen— or should I say unlucky? Then men and women were divided into two groups. Each man was given a child's bow and rubber-tipped arrow, transforming us into oversized cupids. The clowns showed us a dance step. We were to chase the women with the bows and arrows while doing a perfectly ridiculous dance. The women were to flee while dancing a different step. The steps involved rocking back on each foot while moving forward. My face flushed with embarrassment, and I hadn't even begun to dance.

The clowns started drumming and singing wildly. They motioned for us to begin. The crowd convulsed with laughter as we rocked back and forth. Most of us were red-faced but smiling. One walker was taking the dance seriously, his expression intent and focused. This made me smile even more and lose my nervousness. It was all a joke, and at our expense. Was this another test—to see if we could laugh at ourselves? After the intense period we had just had on the walk, the Hopi clowns brought relief.

After the dance, the clowns escorted us back to our seats, rewarding us with rolled-up, paper-thin blue corn cakes called "piki." We were also given store-bought loaf bread and sweet rolls. We shared them with people around us. One elder Hopi politely refused the loaf bread. "That's white man's bread," he said, his brown, full-moon-shaped face frowning. Many Hopi still bake their own bread in outdoor ovens. His refusal was indicative of criticism that the dances, and Hopi culture, have become increasingly contaminated with Western ways.

"Some Hopi come to dance," another elder told me, "but they don't go through the preparation or purification beforehand. And some don't know the reason why they are dancing any more. There are not many who still grow corn."

From the kachina dances, we shuttled to our camp on the Navajo Reservation, only to be invited to an all-night Native American Church ceremony being held in a nearby teepee. Ten of us accepted, the event being a first for many in the group. Our appearance was an obvious shock to late-arriving Navajo attendees. One man jumped back in surprise when he entered the teepee, but, as time passed, differences didn't seem to matter.

This ceremony was the final one in a series of four, the primary purpose of which was to mourn for a son who had been lost in a car wreck. The fire burned brightly for prayers and songs, all of them in the Navajo tongue. Chants echoed around the teepee. Sometimes, it was difficult to tell who was singing; the lips of people barely moved. Some of the walkers began to slouch, it being difficult to focus on prayer and to sit up before a hot fire all night. But, as morning crept closer, an air of celebration pervaded.

John, a walker, was allowed to sing a song that had come to him early in the walk: "You've got to bend your bow, let the energy flow. . . ." Then a Navajo woman prayed over water for all of us, and sunlight soon dazzled through the teepee door. A feast of lamb, fry bread, vegetables, and sweets followed. In the telling of jokes and stories, we shared the medicine of laughter.

The occasion brought to mind one of Raven's prophecies for the walk: "The peyote will look at you in the Four Corners." It seemed obvious to everyone that Raven had been referring to the Native American Church ceremony we had just attended. We were now in that area of the Four Corners, the term for where four states—Colorado, Arizona, New Mexico, and Utah—join together. Traditionally, Native American peoples have recognized it as a place of powerful, spiritual energy. The Navajo people mark its boundaries with four sacred peaks: Blanca Peak to the east; Mount Taylor to the south; San Francisco Peak to the west; and Mount Hersperus to the north. Traditional Hopi consider it to be the center of the world. They deliver offerings and prayers at shrines they have established on several mountains in the area, viewing them as gateways to the spirit realm. Hopi elders are quick to point out, however, that the entire earth is sacred, not just one specific place.

Watching my companions at the feast, I recalled a vision I had had at the nearby Aztec Ruins when visiting with Bear Heart. It had revealed that, after years of violence, light-skinned people would begin to share spiritually with

Native Americans. Bear Heart had spoken of this as well. It was gratifying to feel that we walkers were part of that movement.

Our Navajo host took us to Tuba City to look for a bus or truck that our group could buy for a support vehicle. We had no luck, but he did show us an area where foot-long dinosaur tracks were preserved in a flat bed of stone. "The Navajo say not to mess around with the tracks or a lizard might bite you some day," he said. The tracks were a glimpse into the distant past, a tangible link to images of huge three-toed reptiles lumbering across a prehistoric riverbed or shoreline.

Some tracks had been cut out of the rock, perhaps as an ornament for someone's patio. I wondered about the perpetrators' luck with lizards. Too often, people seek to possess items of antiquity to boost their self-esteem in the present, even if those items have been torn away from their rightful owners or dwelling place.

As we began walking—late, of course—Indian songs and music reverberated through our heads. No dinosaurs were spotted, but they wouldn't have surprised us. We were experiencing much more than we had anticipated. My faith in coming to Indian country was being restored. The walk itself and the example we were striving to set were the necessary bridge in our effort to link our two cultures, Indian and non-Indian.

Chapter
11

KOYAANISQATSI

Our prophecies describe life in the last stages of this earth's cycle," said elder Thomas Banyacya at a Hopi mental health conference we attended. "They speak of a gourd full of ashes that will fall on the ground twice [i.e., the bombs that were dropped on Hiroshima and Nagasaki]. They speak of three forces that will shake up the world. Two have already occurred—that of the Germans and the Japanese [an ancient Hopi tablet at Oraibi clearly shows a swastika inside of a sun sign]. The third force will be that of many people who come in red hats and cloaks. . . . The last days will be dark; people will rain from the sky and then divide good and evil. The level of destruction will depend on how well people harmonize with the environment and share in true brother- and sister-hood, on how well they turn away from a self-centered path. . . ." We didn't understand all of what Banyacya said, such as people raining from the sky, but we assumed he was talking about an archetypal battle.

Banyacya continued, "Our prophecies were written on three stone tablets. One was taken by a man long ago whose skin has since turned white. It will be brought back by this white man who will not lie or cheat. He will fill in the missing piece of the tablets."

I assumed that this splitting of the tablets had occurred long ago. But I was unclear about whether this "white man" was supposed to reincarnate and bring back the missing tablet, or whether he was symbolic of a group or movement of light-skinned people. The part about the missing tablet did seem literal, since the Hopi often communicated prophecy by carving petroglyphs on large rocks.

According to Banyacya, traditional Hopis strive to set a good example of living in harmony. "Hopis keep eyes open in meditation to commune with the environment," he said. "We try to take care of everything and never to destroy the Mother—we don't cut or fence her. We work for things—we avoid throw-aways and instant everything. There's a consequence for every action; we look at the source from where things come. Self-control is a must. Being Hopi means being very strong in order to be peaceful and gentle."

Banyacya believes that Hopi land is a sacred energy center for the Mother Earth and Great Spirit and that its preservation is necessary for the world's preservation. Hopi prayers, ceremonies, and struggles are for all of existence, he attested, lamenting thereby the fading of Hopi traditional life.

Interestingly, the only ones listening to Banyacya's talk were the members of our group. Perhaps the Hopis in the audience had heard it all before, or perhaps some disagreed. There have been many splits in Hopi society, as outlined, for instance, by Frank Waters' *Book of the Hopi*.[1] You can't paint all Hopi with the same broad brush.

The gathering's overall focus was on how Hopi traditional life was bowing to external forces such as materialism and alcoholism, a trend warned about in the prophecies. Fewer acres of land were being farmed each year. Young people were not learning the Hopi language. Customs and values were being lost. Suicides were on the rise. And against the wishes of Hopi spiritual leaders, the nontraditional tribal government was sanctioning the strip-mining of Hopi sacred land at Black Mesa for coal and uranium.

As part of the program, we watched the premiere of a movie called *Koyaanisqatsi*, a Hopi word for "life out of balance," introduced at the conference by its director, Godfrey Reggio. Without words, it depicted the rapid motion and pollution of city life, exaggerated by accelerated photography and spiced with references to Hopi prophecy. The scenes were far removed from the day-to-day living of most of the Hopis. The images we saw of twelve-lane, rush-hour traffic must have seemed like something from another planet to someone raised on an Arizona mesa top.

We were learning at the conference, moreover, that life could be "out of balance" on many levels—mental, physical, and spiritual. The breakup of the traditional family, the trend away from an agrarian lifestyle, the rise in alcoholism and domestic violence, and the dilution of meaningful values were all trends that affected the Hopi as well as the outside world. Environmental degradation, stemming from a lack of respect for or understanding of the natural world, was often the result. During the workshop summaries, a Hopi speaker lamented the fact that few Hopis now make walking pilgrimages to Hopi sacred sites around the Four Corners area. "Today, we have a group of non-Hopi visitors who are walking all the way to Washington, D.C.!" he concluded, hoping that our example would help motivate his people. As we in our group were learning, the slow pace of walking helped one attune with Mother Earth and innate spiritual forces much better than did whizzing by in insulated vehicles of steel and rubber. Walking could be a sacred act in itself, as the Hopi speaker knew.

After the conference, some of us toured the mesa-top city of Oraibi. Having existed for two thousand years or more, it is believed to be the oldest inhabited city in the United States. Here, the scene looked little different than the way it would have appeared centuries ago, with ancient adobe and rock houses and small farm plots stretching into the desert below. Shards of the pottery that once had made Oraibi famous littered the roads. Many were fire orange or sunset yellow, with exquisite designs. The ruins of a church, centuries old, was mute testimony to Christianity's failed foothold. And noticeably absent from the city were electric and water lines; the residents wanted it that way. Those Hopi who chose a more modern path lived below the mesa in the town of Kykotsmovi, or in other towns on or near the reservation.

In the semi-traditional village of Hotevilla, a small contingent visited Grandfather David, a 105-year-old spiritual leader whom his people called the "Pope of the Hopi." He had shared Hopi prophecy around the world and been awarded the Medal of Peace by the United Nations. Now he stayed closer to home. Amazingly clear-minded for his age, he stressed how the walk represented the kind of action needed in the world, being a down-to-earth event that promoted people-to-people communication. "I would like for us to host an international peace gathering on Hopi land," he said, "but I don't know if we can feed everyone. That's our custom—to feed visitors."

Looking out over the Hopi's land, I thought of the peace conference Grandfather David envisioned. These modest people had much to share with the world, especially about establishing a sacred trust with a land that, while it seemed dry and lifeless on the surface, harbored spiritual riches. Given the physical hardships we walkers had endured, we felt we could now better understand the Hopi.

Amid short, blessed sprinkles of rain, we walked up a dirt road to Big Mountain, part of the Navajo-Hopi Joint Use Area. As we had learned before the walk from Navajo elder women in San Francisco, this area was currently the subject of a heated dispute between the two tribes. The controversy centers around Hopi anxiety over the encroaching numbers of Navajo people on their land, a possible outcome being that the Navajo would be subject to relocation. Traditional elders such as Thomas Banyacya and Grandfather David, however, were opposed to forced relocation. They felt the dispute could be resolved by less drastic means. What's more, they maintained that the underlying impetus for the relocation was coming from large energy corporations and certain tribal leaders who sought to rip coal and uranium resources from the land. In looking upon the unspoiled hills of piñon pine and sagebrush, I had difficulty imagining immense mechanical shovels creating pits in the earth as large as towns, while house-sized trucks hauled away minerals.

If the energy argument was true, then the conflict was between the traditional native lifestyle and the consumptive desires of contemporary Western society, not two native tribes. The same thing had occurred when gold had been discovered in northern Georgia, California, and the Black Hills, and when oil had been found in Alaska and Amazonia. Our own lifestyles always affect such situations, in which the choice is often between wastefulness and conservation, dead-end energy alternatives and renewable resources. To take the ecological path often means bucking mass-media advertising and societal programming. It means stepping outside the system to look in with innovative eyes.

The Big Mountain Survival Camp, where we stayed, was founded by the American Indian Movement and several local elders. The camp, nestled in unspoiled green hills amid traces of ancient Anasazi culture, was a budding community. Native American activists, mostly from northern Plains tribes, slept on bunk beds in a small building. Other buildings included a round house for dancing and singing and a cook shack. Young camp residents had stocked up on food in preparation for a long fight or siege. They vowed to resist confiscation of livestock, fencing of the land, and an injunction against new home building among the Navajo. It was a bureaucrat's worst nightmare. The Big Mountain scene was a potential war zone; it made me uneasy.

"What does your culture have to offer?" a Navajo activist challenged, glaring at us. "Mom and apple pie? Burger King? Our culture is with our land. We will fight for it!"

We found more common ground with the activists at evening sweat-lodge ceremonies, where we prayed and smoked the pipe together. Afterward, we cooled ourselves with the night sand, the camp being without running water. I was developing a new respect for that coarse sand. In the spirit of Geronimo, native people were willing to spill blood for it, their own as well as that of others.

Some walkers stayed with nearby Navajo families, helping them plant corn, tend sheep, and chop wood. They became so enamored that they planned to stay behind for several days. I was envious of them, but I felt a need to remain with the walk until we worked out our support-vehicle situation. We were currently searching to buy a suitable pick-up truck, and time was running out for us to find an alternative to backpacking most of our gear.

As our main group left Big Mountain, Navajo elder Catherine Smith led us by foot on a cross-country "short cut." She wore a long dress, deep blue like the evening sky. Her neck was adorned with silver and turquoise jewelry. She was at least seventy years old, yet it was hard to keep up with her.

Catherine guided us through deep washes, small farms, and sheep pastures and past octagonal wood-and-mud hogans. At different times, the air was filled with aromas of sage, wood smoke, and manure. This was Catherine's life-long neighborhood. She knew everyone we passed. Clearly, she did not want to leave her land. She was openly bitter toward the tribal and federal governments for trying to remove her family and neighbors. We had to strain to hear her, mainly because we were struggling to keep up.

"To me," Catherine said, "the white in the American flag represents the white people. The red represents our Indian blood, and each star represents Indian nations who have fallen."

Then she relayed what has become a familiar story among Native Americans: "My youngest daughter has no desire to be a traditional Navajo woman. She wants to go to college in Washington State!" But even as many such young natives are moving into the mainstream, I gathered from Catherine that more non-Indians are also showing a heightened interest in Navajo traditions, increasingly attempting to go beyond the tourist level of viewing roadside trinkets. The question is, How can we balance this cultural and spiritual exchange without further diffusing native cultures? The mere presence of, say, five hundred non-Indians at a traditional ceremony wouldn't be sufficient to keep the native young people at home. And if they all left the reservations to seek the American dream, traditional cultures would shrivel and die. My hope was that the growing non-Indian interest in native ways, such as our walk represented, could help young Native Americans cherish what they have, even as they venture into mainstream Western culture.

The next day, a Navajo medicine man named Edgar stopped us on the road to Piñon, Arizona. He was returning home from an all-night healing ceremony. "What does that staff you're carrying mean to you?" he asked.

"It is like our prayer flag," I replied. "It helps us to pray and it helps guide us." He seemed satisfied.

Many persons of our background would have viewed the staff as an ornamental object to be hung on a wall or placed in a museum. Indeed, one non-Indian man stuck in traffic had called to us, pointing to the staff as we walked past. "Hey, how much do you want to sell that thing for?"

"It's not for sale," several walkers had answered at once. The idea of selling the staff had never occurred to us. It had become a sacred vessel, helping to clear the way for our safe passage through many lands. If the staff had ended up in a museum or private collection, I imagine we would have felt the same anguish native people experience when their sacred objects are placed behind glass. Even their ancestors' graves are robbed in the insatiable quest for artifacts. The resurgent interest in native culture needs to inspire a spiritual search that results in lifestyle changes, not just a greedy search for beautiful and valuable objects. Some things shouldn't be for sale.

After we had exchanged the usual questions and answers about the walk, Edgar concluded: "You are traveling a long ways through many areas. Please do not forget what you have seen here and the problems at Big Mountain. Many of the people there are in anguish. Help spread their message across the country; let those who are unaware know the truth about what's going on. God bless you." Edgar, as did many others along the way, reinforced our sense of purpose. Sometimes, we felt as if we were walking on eagle wings, our spirits were so high.

That evening, two of our walkers, Mikel and Robert Glenn, showed up with a sturdy truck for a permanent support vehicle. Purchased with money we had all pooled, the truck was symbolic of how we could cooperate as a group. We set to work in a celebratory mood, building plywood sides along the truck bed and painting an eagle symbol on one side and a map of our route on the other. It was a proud day.

As we continued through Navajo country with the aid of our new truck, a walk contingent attended the first Navajo conference on uranium-mining casualties. Many of the attendees were widows and fatherless children of mining victims. For decades, miners and people living near the mines had been exposed to unsafe levels of radiation. One 1959 report found radiation levels in some mines at ninety times the acceptable limit. A study of Navajo miners who had worked at the Shiprock mine until 1970 found that 133 of 150 miners had died of lung cancer or various forms of fibrosis ten years later.

Moreover, a tailing dam had burst at Church Rock on the reservation in 1979, sending millions of gallons of contaminated waste into the Rio Puerco River. It was the largest such accident in United States history. As of this writing in 2006, the water is still unsafe.

Since the walk, uranium miners and their families have received some monetary compensation, and the Navajo Nation barred further uranium mining and processing on their lands in 2005. To this day, though, hundreds of old uranium mines and tailings still lay exposed to wind and rain. The Four Corners area suffers the notoriety of having one of the highest radioactivity levels in the United States.

After the conference, I took a side trip, hitchhiking into Colorado to do some advance work. One driver I met shrugged off uranium-associated health problems in favor of higher priorities. "The reason I'm here is that I can make eighteen dollars an hour as a load operator at the mines," he said.

Other non-Indians in the border towns gave me their perspectives on Native Americans. Said one young man, "A 'prairie nigger' is a smart-ass young alcoholic Indian. We don't call the old proud ones that. There are 'prairie niggers' and Indians, just as there are 'honkies' and white people."

Another Caucasian man added, "See all those new pick-up trucks those Indians have? You and I are the ones paying for them with our tax money. I think the Indians should just have to assimilate with the rest of society. None of this reservation crap."

The contrast between this man's view and those of the people with whom I had been walking was a bit shocking. But my biggest shock occurred when I arrived in downtown Denver, far away from the spacious, sculpted land of the Hopi and Navajo. Two persistent African-American drug dealers accosted me, flashing white powder in a baggie. Perhaps my beard, soiled clothes, and backpack misled them. "C'mon man, c'mon man, it's really good," they persisted.

"C'mon man . . ." As the traffic screeched before the looming skyscrapers and my lungs labored in the heavy polluted air, my thoughts kept returning to that Hopi word, *koyaanisqatsi*: "life out of balance."

Chapter 12

LAKOTA COUNTRY

After crossing Colorado's Rockies, suffering through Denver's congestion, and enjoying the wide-open Wyoming plains, we entered the Black Hills of South Dakota, sacred land to the Lakota Sioux and other Plains tribes. In the Fort Laramie Treaty of 1868, the United States government had promised them this land in perpetuity, a result of the only protracted conflict ever won by Native Americans. But the victory had been short-lived. Four years later, traces of gold were found in a Black Hills creek, instigating a flood of gold miners. Fighting ensued, and the Indians subsequently lost the Black Hills.

Today, however, many Native Americans still hold the government to their 1868 promise. The Lakota tribe was awarded a court-ordered settlement of $17.5 million for the land in 1979, but the tribe refused to take it. When we were talking with three Lakota men who visited our camp near Cascade Falls, one of them explained, "We told them we didn't want the money. We want our Black Hills back!" The unclaimed award continues to accrue interest.

As the Lakota men's dusty truck rumbled down the road toward the Pine Ridge Reservation, I gazed upon silhouettes of hills and trees against a night sky and listened to sweet, gurgling water from a nearby stream. What better church than this, where one could feel eternal and at peace, in touch with what one's life can become? No wonder the Lakota hadn't wanted to sell. How can one put a price on beauty, water, mountains, trees, or a tranquil feeling?

Three of us drove ahead to do advance work and explore Lakota country further. We entered the Pine Ridge Reservation, home of the Oglala band of the Lakota Sioux. We soon picked up a Lakota woman named Jeanette and her two young children. Jeanette served as our guide through her land, first taking us high on Porcupine Hill to the KILI radio station, a Lakota-run station with a hundred-mile radius or more. There we did a live interview.

At the nearby town of Wounded Knee, we drove into a dilapidated government housing project to meet with Leola, a local organizer. In her thirties and seven months pregnant, Leola displayed a calm nature and a look that suggested she was good at perceiving nonverbal messages. On her walls were photos of ancestors—Lakota in full regalia on horseback wearing eagle-feather headdresses with teepees in the background. She called one woman in a faded photograph "grandmother" in a tone that suggested she still knew her.

The numerous friends and relatives who dropped by appreciated our hostess's constantly brewing coffeepot and chocolate cake. One friend was Charlotte Black Elk, a descendent of the famous Lakota prophet. She was light skinned for a Lakota, with long black hair and an air of intensity. As had other Lakota we had met, she spoke openly about her past and about the plight of her people.

"I was sent to a government boarding school at age six," she began. "Most of us didn't know English until the end of the year. When the worst student finally spoke it, my teacher was so happy she cried. A lot of parents then came to school and asked this teacher if she wished for one of their children to die, since Sioux people only cry when there is a death. The school administrators replaced that teacher the next year. Now, most of our schools are bilingual, teaching both Sioux and English, so we've come a long way."

If we had arrived a few years earlier, it would have been difficult to interact with Wounded Knee residents. Throughout most of the 1970s, the reservation had been a war zone. Shootouts, murders, and blockaded roads were commonplace. Government buildings had been sandbagged and armed with gun turrets. The Federal Bureau of Investigation and the Oglala tribal government "goon squad" were on one side, and the American Indian Movement was on the other. The fight was partly over reservation mining and grazing leases and partly over the selling of Indian land by the tribal government. Thousands of Lakota people, including Wounded Knee residents, had been caught in the middle, with the local homicide rate rising higher than in most large U. S. cities.

The American Indian Movement had occupied Wounded Knee for seventy-one days. The conflict ended when the two sides agreed on several conditions: a presidential commission review of hundreds of past treaties between the

United States and Indian tribes, especially the 1868 Fort Laramie Treaty; removal of the Oglala Tribal Council and the Bureau of Indian Affairs superintendent; recognition of a traditional Oglala tribal government; and a federal investigation into Oglala tribal president Dick Wilson and his armed squad known as the GOONS (Guardians of our Oglala Nation), about which more than a thousand civil rights complaints had been filed. In the course of events few, if any, of these demands were met, although congressional hearings were conducted on the issues that had led to the confrontation. Several hundred AIM members had been arrested, but most were eventually acquitted or released.

After the occupation, the situation had become even tenser on the reservation and at Wounded Knee, as the civil war continued between traditional people and tribal government supporters. "We knew every car around here," said Leola, "so if someone strange came in, we were aware of it. The women used to meet in secret to discuss things."

At the heart of the matter, Charlotte said, was that the government simply wanted the remaining Lakota land. "We've been pressured to leave for a long time," she went on. "My non-Indian high school guidance counselor used to tell me to marry a white man and get off the reservation. Counselors told the men to get off the reservation, too, and find work. The government agents called it 'economic opportunity.' They were hoping that if enough of us moved off the reservation, the government could take it over. They put our people in trade schools, mostly in plumbing, but when the men went to other towns and cities, the unions wouldn't let them in."

Leola sought to keep her people on their land, so she attacked high unemployment and poverty by facilitating food, clothing, and tool donations through various organizations. Because of this help, new emphasis was being placed on gardening, log-cabin building, and raising wild horses and bison, in a blending of traditional and modern cultures. "We don't want to sell our land," Leola said, echoing a sentiment we had heard on all the reservations. "We'd rather be poor than to sell our Mother."

Bidding Leola goodbye for the time being, the other scouts and I returned to our group and walked the last two miles of the day with them under sunset skies. Several young Lakota joined us, having heard us on the radio. A middle-aged Lakota man named Shorty led us to a camp near the town of Oglala, where unknown assailants had killed two FBI agents. Shorty's former house had been shot up in the process. Faded and empty, it stood before us like a porous skeleton, riddled with bullet holes. A Lakota / Anishinabe man named Leonard Peltier was eventually convicted in the FBI slayings, even though he had not been in the area at the time, according to Shorty. Peltier is serving a life prison sentence; his case has become a rallying cry for the Indian movement.

Shorty added that he, too, had been out of town at the time of the incident; nevertheless, the authorities had also picked him up because of his support of AIM. "For six months, I was held in custody and shipped to Denver, Cheyenne, Fort Collins, and El Paso. Not even my lawyers could find me." He was eventually cleared of suspicion, though, and has been dedicated to the movement ever since, performing legal research for the Peltier case and others.

"We have suffered a lot," Shorty said sadly, "especially in Wounded Knee, Oglala, and Porcupine, so whenever we get a support group here, we don't care what they look like. We make them feel at home." He stared silently into the fire; I felt the pain and sorrow of his people. At an adjacent powwow ground and sun-dance circle, the people held ceremonies for Leonard Peltier in which they tried to take on some of his suffering. The idea, I gathered, is that feeling another's pain better enables one to act on that person's behalf. Perhaps that was ultimately why we walkers had come.

Some activists have said that the Lakota Reservation needs a Marshall Plan to turn around its dire situation. As of 2002, life expectancy there was the lowest in the Western Hemisphere outside of Haiti, hovering at around fifty years of age. Infant mortality is twice the national average. About half of the reservation children live below the poverty level, while more than half of reservation houses are substandard. Two out of three reservation students drop out of high school. Traditional ways and ceremonies such as the sun dance are gaining ground in an attempt to stem the tide, but outside help is also needed. Organizations such as the Friends of Pine Ridge Reservation help to publicize needs and funnel aid appropriately.

The next morning at camp, Shorty held up a striking, blue-denim beaded vest. "My granddaughter made this for me when she was only thirteen," he said in a halting voice. "I am very proud of it. In our culture, if we find we are becoming too attached to something, we give it away." With a weak smile, he placed the vest in my hands. I was speechless.

Ironically, at the time I was proudly wearing a finely woven vest my uncle Bear Heart had given me two years before. "This is yours," he had said, holding it out to me. "If you want to give it away to someone else, that is up to you. There are no strings attached." I had cherished that vest ever since, it being one of the few remaining material gifts from my uncle. But what I carried in my heart, I now realized, was much richer. Even though Shorty did not expect a return gift for his vest, he seemed pleased when I presented him with mine. Beyond the beautiful piece of beadwork, he had given me something of immense value—a good lesson.

That day our whole group walked the same road to Wounded Knee on which the other scouts and I had driven the day before. At one point, an old Lakota man greeted us at the roadside. "That bluff over there is holy," he said, pointing a wrinkled finger to a round, white bluff against a backdrop of sparsely vegetated hills. "The medicine men go there to pray. They've been going there for a long time. If you put your hands on the bluff, you will be healed."

With the elder's permission, four walkers in need of healing visited the bluff. When a Lakota elder says such a thing, one does not take it lightly. Our bluff contingent soon returned with a good report.

"My back hasn't felt this good in months," exclaimed a walker named Coyote, "and Leslie's throat swelling has visibly gone down." I was not skeptical, as I had seen similar results from Native American medicine. Considering the thousands of years during which these people had flourished before the advent of European-introduced diseases, we had much to learn from them. In some ways, by comparison, all of us were still "babies."

In Pine Ridge, the largest reservation town, we stopped at a grocery store where a drunken man asked me for money. After I gave him some change, he wept on my shoulder. "I've been sleeping in a haystack for four nights," he said. Other Lakota crowded around us, asking questions. Most of them were friendly, but I was glad Shorty was present. We were like guppies in a fish bowl. Of particular interest were the tall, plywood panels fastened to our truck. A painted eagle framed by a rainbow peered at onlookers on one side, and a map of our route was splashed across the other. Every hundred miles or so, we would fill in the dots on the map to indicate the completion of another portion of our route. The Lakota country was one section I hoped we wouldn't finish too quickly.

That evening at Wounded Knee, we shared a dinner with Leola and other residents. This warm occasion was far different from the AIM occupation of that place in 1973, not to mention the massacre that had occurred there over a century before. The story goes that, in 1890, a Lakota chief named Big Foot and his people had left their reservation to ghost dance at Wounded Knee. There they had prayed and danced for the return of their lost lands and warriors. Then soldiers had come. A scuffle had ensued. The soldiers had opened fire on unarmed men, women, and children. More than two hundred Indian dead had been buried in a mass grave just above our camp. Now, I could feel their curious eyes upon us. That night, their ghostly images danced around the powwow grounds. Any sleep I had was brief.

History can be difficult to grasp emotionally, especially when part of it still exists on a spiritual level. Perhaps this spiritual level needs healing first; it begs for a peaceful resolution. No wonder some of Big Foot's descendants are restless.

Shortly after sunrise, Leola led us up a pine-covered hill west of our camp. Dew-covered grass soaked our feet. None of us cared. The morning was spectacular. Cool breezes tickled treetops into rustling melodies. Cheerful meadowlarks filled the air. A majestic, red-tailed hawk soared high above; we followed its piercing cry as we climbed the hill.

An elder medicine man, a Lakota named Zach, greeted us on the hill's summit. He was husky, almost bear-like. His loose, gray hair glistened in the early light. Although he did not speak English, he greeted us with a warm smile.

Glancing around Zach's hilltop home, I determined that, while Indian medicine has its own rewards, material wealth was not one of them. His ramshackle cabin was a place I wouldn't want to occupy during a north Florida cold snap, much less a life-threatening winter in South Dakota. Junked automobiles littered the yard. Chickens bobbed about under the watchful eye of several cats. Summer grass stood tall and wild looking.

We stood quietly around a roaring fire that heated rocks for the upcoming sweat-lodge ceremony. Would a Lakota sweat be different from other sweats? Each one, thus far, had been unique.

Zach sent the men into the lodge for the first sweat. Shorty shoveled in crimson-hot rocks. The door flap closed. The old man cleared his throat and prayed and sang in the Lakota tongue. Then we sat in darkness, listening to our breathing and the singing birds. Steam hissed from the glowing rocks as Zach ladled on water. I wasn't sure if anyone else was supposed to speak. Perhaps the rocks were to speak first.

Finally, Zach broke the silence. Shorty interpreted his Lakota words for us. "An old chief we haven't heard from in a long time has come to be with you for the rest of your journey," Zach began. "Do not be afraid. Do not stray from your path, and you will achieve your goals. You will pass through many briars, but stay focused. Be not afraid of the thunder beings, for they are with you. You will see things you never believed existed. This I know. I come as the coyote at night."

The old man had spoken slowly and deliberately, but with great strength and firmness. We smoked the pipe with him and then bathed in dawn's light. It was the shortest sweat ceremony in which I had participated, and one of the most profound.

The women entered the sweat lodge next. It wasn't long before they, too, were finished. In silence, we walked back to camp. The morning seemed even more beautiful and pure. We held hands in a big circle and prayed for the healing of the land and its people. The women had received a similar message from Zach; they were equally awed by the profound and eloquent nature of his simple words.

Native American leaders of the past were renowned for awe-inspiring statements and speeches. Zach lived up to that reputation. Now, something new seemed to be happening—a spiritual sharing between cultures—and we were proud to participate in it.

Later that morning, Shorty continued to guide us through Lakota country. He spoke about the Lakota ways, especially the sun dance: "The main difference between our religion and Christianity is that we talk directly to the Great Spirit, while the Christians go through Jesus. The basic principles are similar. We both believe in suffering, except that Christians allow Christ to suffer for them, while all of us seek to suffer ourselves for our people.

"They couldn't build a cross big enough for all the Lakota to fit on, so we have the sun dance where we pierce our bodies with a sharp bone or piece of wood and attach ourselves by a thong to a center pole. We have to prepare all year for this event, fasting a day or two every month. During the sun dance, we fast for eight days straight; on the last day, we spill our blood.

"Around the center pole are twenty-eight poles which make up a circle. Each of these poles represents a medicine or element we need to live on. We call everything we need for life a medicine. We have symbols for everything. The color blue, for example, represents the sky and all that flies, and the water and all that swims. The color purple represents all of the insects—they have an important place, too—and so on."

He pointed out two medicinal plants along the roadside: bitterroot for coughs and blood clotting, chokecherry for quenching thirst. He said that this type of traditional knowledge was rarely being passed down now, as most young people were not motivated to receive it.

"A farmer with a lot of hay to work came to a nearby housing development the other day looking for help," Shorty lamented, "but none of the young people would go with him because the government gives them money. When I was young, we'd have to find work."

Increasingly, I was realizing that job programs are more important for well-being than simple welfare, if people are capable of working. Having a job promotes responsibility and leaves less idle time for drinking, which is a monumental problem on the reservations, especially when monthly government checks arrive.

After a twenty-seven-mile day, we arrived at our camp in Swett, South Dakota, population nine. We were walking longer distances to make up for a scheduling mistake I had made and to allow more time for days off. A vanload of Native Americans stopped, curious about what we were doing. They were returning from a cross-country relay run from New York to Los Angeles to honor the great Indian athlete Jim Thorpe. Having traversed numerous reservations, they sought recognition of Thorpe and the unification of their people. We posed for photographs together; everyone felt that our meeting was more than mere coincidence.

Our whirlwind tour continued the next day. After walking twelve miles, we shuttled off the route to meet Charlotte Black Elk, whom the other scouts and I had met earlier at Wounded Knee. Charlotte had invited us to an occasion where two ceremonies were to take place— "Releasing the Spirit" and "Throwing the Ball." They were to be held in an open, grassy field surrounded by forested hills. The elder Black Elk had lived in the area. We walkers were the first to arrive. Buzzards soared lazily over distant treetops on a warm, sunny afternoon.

Slowly, on "Indian time," Lakota people began to appear, about two hundred in all. As we did not see Charlotte, we were feeling out of place. But soon Zach showed up in an old sedan, smiling and nodding when he saw us. Then Charlotte and others drove in, pulling a long horse trailer. Our excitement started building.

Zach motioned for everyone to make a wide circle. Sage was burned. With its purifying smoke permeating the air, Charlotte handed out copies of Black Elk's descriptions of the two ceremonies. Few would have known them otherwise, as these rituals are not often observed in modern times.

Zach slowly stepped into the circle's center. Praying aloud in Lakota, he first raised a pipe to the sky, followed by a huge, painted buffalo skull. Then he raised a buckskin bag and a painted box. The bag, which had been kept in the box, contained some hair of Charlotte's father, Black Elk's son, who had died a year before. By this means, her father's soul was believed to have been contained in the box, so that it could be purified in preparation for meeting Wakan-Tanka, a collective term for the spirits of all beings, or The Great Spirit. According to Black Elk's teachings, the soul had to be kept this way for a year in a pure place by one who led a clean lifestyle—by a person, that is, with good thoughts, prayers, and deeds. In return for this help, the rest of the people gained knowledge from the purifying soul. Hence, all life on earth benefited in the process.

In a type of communion service, a glowing pipe was passed around the circle, followed by buffalo meat and chokecherry juice that represented the body and blood of the man. Then, the box was opened and the soul released. Several onlookers wept for joy. The soul was now free to travel the spirit path to the Milky Way, attaining union with Wakan-Tanka. The entire spirit world was supposed to rejoice, and, by the tingling I felt, I believed it to be true.

So unusual was this ceremony to missionaries that it was outlawed by the United States government in 1890; a date was set whereby all souls had to be released.

Personally, I liked the ritual of releasing a soul better than that of burying a body. The mood was different than at most funerals, as there seemed to be an understanding and appreciation of the spirit world and of the two-way benefits that can occur.

For the next ceremony, Charlotte's four-year-old daughter was brought to the circle's center. Zach handed her a red-and-blue buffalo skin ball, about the size of a child's fist. According to Black Elk's written description, the red represented the world and the blue the heavens; thus, heaven and earth were united in the ball. The young girl symbolized the beginning stage of life, the first of four, and she also represented the Mother Earth and the generations to come. She was to throw the ball to all four directions and then straight up—to Wakan-Tanka. Only a few in the crowd would be able to catch the ball. They represented the few people in life—though many strive for it—who reach a special closeness with Wakan-Tanka and achieve *wahupa*, enlightenment.

With the painted buffalo skull, Zach gently nudged the girl toward the crowd gathering in the west. With help from her older sister, she raised her arm and threw the ball. A mad scramble ensued. The ball was batted down; it rolled across the ground. People dove and jostled for it as if it were a winning home-run ball hit into the bleachers. Finally, a young man gave a yelp and emerged from the clutch. He held out the ball toward the four directions, and then to the sky and earth, before returning it to the girl. Charlotte brought the smiling young man a gift—a pony! Now I understood: There were more than spiritual riches to be gained.

When the ball was thrown to the north, I tried hard to catch it. It whizzed by like prairie winds. If the ball represented enlightenment, then enlightenment surely could be fleeting. As Black Elk said in *The Sacred Pipe*: "The game as it is played today represents the course of a man's life, which should be spent in trying to get the ball, for the ball represents Wakan-Tanka, or the universe. . . . In the game today it is very difficult to get the ball, for the odds—which represents ignorance—are against you."[1]

Soon a lucky woman held up the north ball. Many in the crowd gave a big yelp. A few moaned. She, too, acknowledged the directions and received a pony.

Next the girl threw the ball to the east, the direction from where the hairy Europeans first emerged onto the continent. It popped from one person's hand to another. No one could grasp it. At last, the ball just fell into the hands of John Montrose, one of our walkers. He hadn't been scrambling for it; he had simply been standing nearby.

Sometimes, enlightenment comes when we are not attached to the outcome.

When a colt was brought to John, we were all smiles. "Hey, John, now you can ride all the way to the East Coast!" I teased.

A young Lakota girl was standing nearby. John handed her the reins. "Here, it is yours," he said to her. The look on the girl's face was one of surprise and disbelief. Onlookers nodded their heads, approving.

There are certain moments that you know at the time you will cherish for the remainder of your life. They may be fleeting—faces, feelings, words, actions—but they can permanently impact who you are and how you relate to the world. When John won that pony—and promptly gave it away—I knew I was in one of those moments. His selfless act reflected positively on us all.

The south direction was next, and another pony was soon given away.

Then the girl threw the ball for the fifth and last time. She threw it straight up, representing the center of the universe. Black Elk said, "It is a little girl, and not an older person, who stands at the center and who throws the ball. This is as it should be, for just as Wakan-Tanka is eternally youthful and pure, so is this little one, who has just come from Wakan-Tanka, pure and without any darkness. Just as the ball is thrown from the center to the four quarters, so Wakan-Tanka is at every direction and is everywhere in the world; and as the ball descends upon the people, so does His power."[2]

Without Black Elk's book, perhaps the ceremony—and its important symbolism—would have been lost.

After the ritual came a feast of corn, chokecherry cobbler, buffalo meat, and buffalo tripe, nearly the entire animal being used to show proper respect. Then Charlotte spoke to us. She wore a striking, black dress adorned with elk teeth and beaded bear-paw designs. "When I was growing up," she began, "I did some of these seven sacred rites of the Sioux with my family, such as the puberty rites. I thought everyone did them, but I later learned that we were about the only ones.

"This ceremony takes the commitment of a whole family. For instance, my daughter has been reared in a special way to prepare her for the ball throwing ritual. Now, I have held all seven of the sacred Sioux ceremonies that my grandfather described. I am finished, but others have now seen them, and so they will continue. We haven't been conducting these ceremonies much because we need a buffalo for them, and the buffalo have been almost extinct. But now they are coming back!"

After we helped Charlotte clean up, she asked if we could give a Lakota grandmother a ride home. "No problem," we replied.

The elderly woman was gentle and had a sweet smile. We helped her climb into Mikel's van, one of our support vehicles; she pointed the way to her house. Her voice was soft and youthful. "I haven't attended this ceremony since I was four years old," she said wistfully. "Then I was the little girl throwing the ball."

Fulfilling Raven's prophecy early in the walk, a contingency of walkers did indeed attend a sun dance in South Dakota. It was a four-day ceremony in honor of Lakota chief and medicine man Frank Fools Crow. Volunteer security guards manned the entrance to the grounds, informing the driver of each vehicle that it was forbidden to take in items such as cameras, tape recorders, alcohol, drugs, or guns. Much to our surprise, one new walker voluntarily gave up some marijuana and a pistol he had stashed in his car.

Word about the incident spread quickly; I could feel gossip seep into the ceremonial throng like blood spilling on thirsty ground. Being non-Indian had already put us under scrutiny, and this event labeled us even more broadly as impure. When medicine pipes were passed, we were often skipped over, avoided as if diseased. An open-mike session in which I addressed the crowd, stating our intent, did little to change the situation. Regardless, while gazing at the center pole, the symbolic tree of life, I envisioned a rainbow of colors spreading throughout the world, reaffirming to me the true meaning of this ceremony—purification and healing.

On the last night of the sun dance, a native man invited us to a Lakota trance ceremony; perhaps he felt sorry for us. Four of us accepted. After dark, we arrived at an old house surrounded by grassy hills. Many Lakota mingled about. Our host was an unassuming, middle-aged Lakota medicine man named Vernal. He reminded me of Eagle Man, someone who didn't stand out upon first meeting.

"We have something going on every night," he said, "sweats, *yuwipi* [a ceremony where the shaman calls the spirits and interprets their messages]. . . . I send people up on the hill for their vision quests all the time. Some might stay for four days, fasting, but most come back in a day or so. I have someone up there now. This ceremony tonight, in fact, is a thank-you that another medicine man, Wallace Black Elk, is giving me because, when he needed help, I sent him up on the hill. He found what he needed.

"Once we start the ceremony, there are seven spirits who usually come. They come in different forms. If you see them, don't touch them. They might send you on a trip for four days and you might not want to come back!" We four walkers squirmed a little.

Around midnight, Wallace arrived. With the rest of the attendees—about forty in all—we filed into a boarded-up mobile home. The structure was empty, so we sat on the floor against the walls; the crowded room quickly became hot and stuffy. Vernal lit a candle and a long-stem pipe and passed it to everyone. Then he extinguished all light, enveloping us in darkness. He and Wallace began pounding on two huge drums, one on each side of the room. Then they sang a spirit chant. Silver sparks shot across the floor. I wondered if others saw them. Suddenly, loud banging noises came from the trailer's metal walls and roof. Wallace and Vernal stopped drumming.

The spirits had arrived.

In an orderly fashion, each person posed one or two questions to the spirits. Vernal's wife interpreted their replies, acting as a medium. Many of the questions and answers were long and personal. Near the end, the medium said to speed things up: "The spirits say that people need air, and that there has been an accident; they need to go to the hospital soon."

When the question-and-answer session was finished, the drumming and singing resumed to announce the spirits' exit and to show thanks. Candles were lit, and we filed out to a great feast under the stars. How long had such pre-dawn feasts been occurring in Lakota country? And where had the spirits gone? It was a night to remember, as was our entire experience on the Lakota reservations.

Coyote, one of our walkers, summed it up: "We seem to have the experience of a lifetime every couple of days. The walk is a means to open many doors." His comment reminded me of something Bear Heart had told me after the Cheyenne sun dance. We had been walking to his camp from the main circle when he leaned over and quietly said, "You will learn all of our ways." The remark confused me and he did not elaborate. But now I wondered if Bear Heart had foreseen the walk and other events.

When we were hitchhiking back to the main walk group, a Winnebago Indian grandmother who boasted of having 230 grandchildren as well as some great-grandchildren drove us fifty miles out of her way. She gave us food and a special spirit rock named "One Who Thunders." It had appeared on her nightstand one morning, she said. I remembered Zach's prophecy during the sweat lodge: "Be not afraid of the thunder beings for they are with you. . . ."

The weather had been blistering hot; we hoped the thunder rock would help bring rain. Several weeks remained of the walk, and more tribes lay ahead.

Chapter
13

MISSOURI RIVER TRIBES

At the beginning of the nineteenth century, the Missouri River country was still unspoiled and wild, and the tribes in the area were in their zenith. It was just at this time that Lewis and Clark ventured into this land, marveling at all they saw. To read their journals is vicariously to relive the adventures found in a lost America that no longer exists. And yet, as we walked parallel to the river, dipping south, we were still able to experience some of this land's timeless beauty. While the soul of America is tarnished, it is not dead, just as is true of her native people.

Neola Walker, chairwoman of the Winnebago tribe, met us on the road. In the 1830s, a large group of her people had been relocated from Wisconsin to a reservation along the Missouri. "Come by our tribal headquarters," she said, "We have lunch all ready for you." She had read about us on the front page of the *Sioux City Journal*, although word had spread to her earlier via the moccasin telegraph.

Upon arriving at the one-story building in the town of Winnebago, we were asked to introduce ourselves to several members of the elected tribal council. Then it was their turn. They described their tribal history and culture and the issues and challenges they were facing now. A few years before, the tribe had won an unprecedented battle over disputed Missouri River land with the Army Corps of Engineers. "Everyone kept telling us that you can't beat the Corps," said Neola, "but we did!"

Neola, a self-proclaimed "schemer," did not have kind words for other government agencies. "We call the BIA [the Bureau of Indian Affairs] 'Bossing Indians Around.' Sometimes, it seems that the government just wants us to sell trinkets along the highway. They have their finger in everything we do. Our goal is self-sufficiency."

The tribe was already working to be owners of their own grocery, mortuary, gas station, bingo parlor, cattle ranches, and other businesses and services, enabling it better to control employment and diffuse the often-inflated reservation prices. At the same time, a new cultural awareness program was reviving tribal traditions, and the Winnebago were seeking more representation on the local school board. While many of us were interested in Native American spirituality, we also realized that a people do not exist separate from their economy. All aspects of tribal life are important.

In the ensuing months, I often thought about that gutsy chairwoman, Neola Walker, and her tribe's struggles. Subsequent to the walk, her people would largely be successful in their drive toward self-sufficiency, opening several businesses, a casino, a tribal college, a hospital, a nursing home, a senior citizen center, a community center, schools, and a youth center. They would also establish a viable bison herd.

We continued our trek to Macy, Nebraska, for the Omaha Indian powwow, a four-day festival of colorful dancing and give-aways. We camped there the first night as guests of the tribe. I had not known of the powwow when setting the itinerary, but, as with many aspects of the walk, the timing was perfect.

Walking up a hill to set up camp above the powwow grounds, I noticed a man slouched against a pickup truck. He sneered at me and then tipped a bottle of gin, taking a long gulp. "Hey you," he called to me, "come over here or I'll slash your throat!" I walked closer, but not within arm's length. My heart beat faster.

"What the hell are you doing here on our land?" he demanded. "Most of you are white. You're treacherous! Why are you always trying to be Indian?"

"We are here to help protect the earth," I answered cautiously, not sure how to answer, "to spread peace and to support your people."

"Naw, come on, why are you really here? You're not Indian. Now, who's the head of this operation?"

"I'm the coordinator of the walk."

He staggered closer. His eyes narrowed. Gin exuded from him, as if giving him his voice. "How much money would your people give me if I held a gun to your head and threatened to blow it off?"

"I doubt they could give you much. We don't have much money." The question almost struck me as funny, although the seriousness of the situation forbade me to laugh. I wasn't sure how to diffuse it.

The man stared at me with a wild gaze. He stuck his face right up to mine. His glazed eyes were filled with confusion and frustration. It was an all-too-familiar look; as was true for many others, his battle for survival had turned in on itself in a slow, desperate movement toward suicide. His search for identity was now confined to a bottle. While concerned for our safety, I also felt pity.

"Man, I could just blow you away!" he boasted.

An Omaha elder was passing by and stepped in between us. "Hey," he told the man in a firm voice, "you go somewhere else and leave these people alone." The man staggered away.

"That's just the way he is when he's drinking," the elder said. "I've tried to help him, but he's got too much anger. Not all of us are like him. I don't care what color you are; you're welcome here. My house is right over the hill there and you are welcome any time. What you people are doing is real good."

I thanked him and glanced over at the drunken man. To my horror, he was clutching a long, unfolded pocketknife and staggering toward our group. Fortunately, two of his friends grabbed him from behind and wrestled away the knife. I began walking down the hill to find the tribal police but stopped cold when a truck door slammed and an engine revved. It was the drunk! Now he was even more dangerous.

Peering menacingly, he popped the truck into gear and floored the gas pedal. The engine's growl turned into a roar. Tires spun. Dirt and grass flew into the air. Wham! The truck bashed into the rear flank of our support van. Barely slowing, it sped down the hill and into a deep ditch. The tribal security police soon rushed in and wrestled the man into a patrol car.

Mikel, the owner of the van, said nothing. His actions spoke loudly, however, when he put his head under a water spigot and turned it on. At least only steel, and not flesh, had been damaged.

It had been fur trappers and traders who first introduced alcohol to most North American native tribes. From the beginning, the object was to get drunk, not to drink socially. Ironically, the Indian Prohibition Action of 1832 only reinforced this model by motivating native people to drink quickly so that they wouldn't be caught with alcohol in their possession. The law was repealed in 1953, but by then the pattern was well established.

Today, alcohol dependence among Native Americans is higher than among any other ethnic group in the United States. As a result, they suffer a high percentage of alcohol-related deaths, suicides, crimes, health problems, and fetal alcohol syndrome.[1]

Studies have, however, poked holes in the theory that Native Americans have a genetic predisposition to alcoholism.[2] More probable factors include the continual erosion of the Indian way of life, poverty, unemployment, welfare dependence, and the loss of traditional Native American spiritual practices. Hope for breaking the cycle of addiction lies in reestablishing a spiritual framework, developing a positive support network, and improving economic conditions.[3]

The evening after our encounter with the drunken man, we attended a free dinner as the opening event of the four-day

Omaha Indian powwow. Attended by around 150 people, the feast was in honor of a young woman whom the tribe had appointed as the powwow princess.

At first, with my adrenaline still pumping from the confrontation with the drunken man, I had to remind myself to breathe—and to smile. When people smiled in return, I began to relax. Then a tribal spiritual leader welcomed us publicly as part of his blessing for the meal, and his sincerity helped further to dispel the recent fracas from our minds.

The dinner was a simple stew, the type we had shared with other native peoples: beef, potatoes, and carrots, cooked in a giant vat. In addition, there was plenty of fresh corn-on-the-cob to go around. For dessert, there was a somewhat tart chokecherry pudding, a Plains favorite.

The entire feast was a give-away meal, being completely sponsored by the family of the young woman to show their appreciation that she had been selected as the princess. The belief, as the elder explained, was that everyone partaking in the give-away would bestow a special blessing on the person being so honored. The custom was similar to that of certain tribal birthday celebrations. At an Omaha Native American birthday party, the ones who receive the presents are the guests!

After the meal, the powwow dancing began, and, when there was a break, I was invited to speak to the tribe. I relayed our purpose and desire to share from the heart, stating that all of us benefited from a mutual understanding of our cultures. Afterward, Coyote repeated to me a conversation he had had with an Omaha man who had wanted to know more about us. "I told him that the walk had come about through a vision of yours," Coyote said, "and the man was surprised. He said he didn't know white people had visions."

Lying down to sleep that night to the music of drums, high-pitched singing, and shaking leg bells, I felt that the hand of friendship had been extended both ways and grasped by each group.

The next morning, an Omaha man came by our camp and introduced himself as one of the tribe's few remaining pipe carriers. He believed in what we were doing. "We are such a small minority," he said. "We need all the help we can get. I've been much more involved in how the tribe operates since I took my last drink six years ago. I've learned how really to communicate with people, and I've learned the power of prayer. Now, I'm a counselor for alcoholics."

I gave him some pure tobacco for his pipe, convinced that his example was an inspiration to others. Perhaps the drunken man from the night before would relay a similar story in the future.

As we began walking through the relatively small reservation, three young Omaha men called from the roadside: "Hey, you, Custer, come over here!" They had singled out Eddy, whose thin frame and long blonde hair and beard contributed to a striking—and unfortunate—resemblance to George Armstrong Custer, that infamous Indian fighter who had grievously miscalculated Indian strength at the Battle of the Little Big Horn. Remembering the previous evening's episode and being cognizant of the original Custer's fate, I thought, "Oh no, not again!"

Eddy returned from talking with the Omaha youths a few minutes later bearing a relieved smile. "They just wanted to know what we were doing," he said. I jokingly urged him to consider a haircut and a shave at the next town.

Both Omaha and Winnebago Indians continued to interact with us at our walk gathering in a downtown Omaha park, set up by a non-Indian organizer, Rhonda Prazan. Rhonda had found out about the walk months before and had offered to help. She volunteered at a local Native American center that provided social services to elderly native people. As water rushed through the park's concrete watercourse, a Winnebago elder gave the opening prayer. Many of us were crying by the end of it; his humility had deeply touched us. By example, native people were teaching many of us how to pray and speak from the heart. I followed the elder by introducing the walk, describing how it had come about as a vision and what our goals were—peace, ecological sanity, and Native American rights. On a basic level, I said, the walk was teaching us how to live more harmoniously with the earth and with each other. We hoped that our example would inspire others. Then we listened intently to the Native American speakers Rhonda had lined up. The only disappointment was that, except for a handful of Native Americans, the audience consisted mostly of walkers sitting on the grass in front of the podium. Still, we didn't want anything to dampen this event on a beautiful, clear morning.

"Nothing can put you in closer contact with nature than to walk this earth," said Fred Buckles, Director of the Office of Indian Education for the Omaha Public Schools. "In trying to live more harmoniously, I think you're reflecting the brotherhood of mankind."

Another Native American speaker, Frank Lamero, added, "I saw you walkers on the road near Homer. So did my daughter. It made an impact on my family to see people who care. You may not see the results of your efforts for a long time, but I think my daughter will remember you and why you are walking in years to come."

A non-Indian speaker, Hazel Rues, represented the Omaha Nuclear Freeze Campaign. "We must be one with the earth and one with each other," she said. "We must listen to the nuclear threat and to the wisdom of the Native American."

After the gathering, an Omaha/Cree woman visited us at the Indian center where we were staying. "I judge if something is good by how it makes me feel inside," she said. "Right now, I feel tingly all over. Here's five dollars!"

Her gift touched us. Even though our brochure mentioned that donations would be accepted to cover group expenses, we never asked for money directly from people we met. Our intent was not to be traveling panhandlers, but support in the form of money, food, or a place to lay our heads was always welcome.

Lewis and Clark had had an ulterior motive for reaching out to native people, that being the expansion of United States territory. Our goals were different. We sought friendship, spiritual truth, and justice for past and present wrongs. My heart told me that the day had been another step on the road to peace among our peoples.

The Heart of America Indian Center in Kansas City had a nice ring to its name. On an advance run, I called the center and immediately set up a gathering and accommodations for the walk group for two nights. "I've expected you for some time," said staff member Jim McKinney, a Potawatomi Indian from Kansas. Surprisingly, Jim had a fat file on the walk, articles having appeared in several Indian newsletters. In 1838, his people had been forcibly relocated from Illinois and Indiana on what was called "The Trail of Death."

Jim explained that thousands of native people live in Kansas City, representing more than fifty tribes. Most major cities in the United States and Canada have similar diverse Native American populations. The center focuses on social services and counseling for alcoholics. It also distributes surplus government food to needy persons of all cultures.

Our gathering at the center was small but intimate. Several Native Americans were present, along with peace and ecology activists from the area. It was the first time representatives from all three factions had come together in Kansas City. We gave a slide show and presentation that covered the journey through South Dakota—highlighting Mono Lake, the relocation of the Big Mountain Navajos, uranium mining, the struggles of the Lakota people, and the many kindnesses that people we had met had bestowed on us—before opening the meeting up for questions and sharing.

"I'm glad that the Indian is part of the focus of your walk, because the Indian seems to be left out of everything," a Native American woman told us, referring to our aim to promote Indian rights and establish a bridge between the two cultures. I wasn't sure of her tribe, since many different ones were represented in the room.

Another native woman added, "This feeling you have in your hearts, we have always felt it. In some ways, you are the Indians, now, too."

We presented Jim McKinney with a walk T-shirt. "I really appreciate the gift," he said, "because in the Indian way, a person has status, not by what he accumulates, but by what he or she gives away."

The Indian Center, in giving us food, shelter, and a place to gather, was a good example of how to put this spiritual principle of the give-away into practice. I also remembered the many other hospitable people we had met on our journey, especially the most materially poor people in the United States—the reservation Indians. On this walk, we had been blessed with countless treasures of the heart that we hoped to be able to pass on to others.

Chapter
14

GATEWAYS

The St. Louis Arch: "Gateway to the West." Reaching that symbolic monument made for a nice break from our ramble past aromatic breweries and bakeries and inner-city storefronts protected by iron bars and chain-link fences. We took time to explore the Museum of Westward Expansion, which stands beneath the arch. The museum's exhibits featured a glorious account of the Lewis and Clark expedition and of the ensuing wagon trains and settlement. A prominent quote by General Philip Sheridan justified the slaughter of the buffalo that deprived Native Americans of their primary food source as a necessary step in westward expansion: "Let them kill, skin, and sell until the buffalo is exterminated, as it is the only way to bring lasting peace and allow civilization to advance."

Notably, though, little attention was given to the lifestyles, culture, viewpoints, or history of the native inhabitants. No mention was even made of the once-thriving native society in St. Louis, the one that had centered around the huge Monk's Mound at Cahokia, just across the river. Over three stories tall, the earthen base is as large as Egypt's Great Pyramid.

Outside the museum, I looked over the Mississippi River lined with industries, smokestacks, barges, and a floating "paddleboat" McDonald's. This urban panorama also marked the "Gateway to the West."

Karen Lewis, our St. Louis hostess, relayed an interesting incident to us: "A friend of mine was asked a trivia question on a game show: 'Who was the first person born on this continent?' The correct answer was the name of a European!" Karen exclaimed. "Sometimes our history assumes that, before Columbus came, there were no real people here." I nodded in agreement. In Florida, St. Augustine is often cited as North America's oldest city, even though Pueblo and Hopi villages, and perhaps settlements of other tribes, were thriving long before the arrival of Europeans.

Karen was involved with a group known as M.A.I.S.— the *Mancomunidad de la America India Solar*—which translates as the "Association of Solar Indian America." (The acronym M.A.I.S. sounds like the Spanish word for corn, *maize*.) Founded in Ecuador in 1977, the group sought to reunite spiritually the native people of North, Central, and South America. Its members had a meeting in which a Mayan man gave a gift to a North American medicine man. "The Mayan was crying," Karen said. "He had been instructed to give this particular gift many years ago, and now the bestowing of it was finally fulfilled."

The group is no longer active, and I have since tried to discover what the gift was without success. But I do know that the group members believed the giving of it symbolized a reunification of the Americas. Even our walk seemed symbolically tied into this idea. Months ago, before the walk had started, a visiting Mayan elder had noted that the route we were to take resembled a snake, which, along with the condor, is a symbol of South America. At the same time, the image we adopted for ourselves was that of the eagle, which is symbolic of North America. So, I was pleased to learn, the concept of reuniting the Americas was imbedded in the very imagery of our journey.

More recently, in 2003, Incan priest Richardo Pecho held a ceremony at the ancient Mayan ruins of Mayapan in Mexico to end five hundred years of oppression and mark the beginning of a new five hundred years of hope for native peoples of North and South America. Pecho said the Incans had prophesized the separation of indigenous peoples due to colonization, but that now is the time "for the reunion of all cultures of the Americas and to awaken the collective subconscious to remember these things."[1] One purpose of the ceremony, attended by native people of both continents, was to restore the balance between male and female energies.

Karen took us to the New World Festival, staged in a St. Louis city park. Its purpose was to promote harmonious living with the earth. The festival began with an opening meditation and prayer, followed by heavenly guitar and piano music. From words spoken at the podium and through several awareness-raising educational booths, we found much focus on environmental protection and healing as well as on relating spiritually to nature. The festival administrators treated us as honored guests, and we felt welcome.

We set up a booth alongside other stands promoting various holistic health practices and spiritual paths. Many of the hundreds of people in attendance were supportive. I began to feel a sense of hope for the large cities, for this "Gateway to the West." Perhaps our destructive societal patterns could be transformed. The seeds of ideas planted in our psyches would, in turn, be manifested in our lifestyles and consumptive habits. They would begin to grow on a small scale and spread out.

By this time on the journey, our own group had undergone a transformation. Morning and evening circles—where we shared personal experiences, songs, prayers, feelings, and logistics—had become so enjoyable that we rarely sought to break them up. Sometimes we practiced a silent focus, wherein the essence of each person seemed to magnify. My own soul was often touched by the group magic, and I frequently sought more than the daily quotient of hugs. Were these the same people who had fought with each other in the Arizona desert and had nearly split apart? We had the same faces, maybe, but we were not the same group. Coyote tried to articulate what was emerging: "It's as if we're foliage in the fall. Everyone is showing their true colors."

Leaving St. Louis, we crossed the Ohio River at the "buffalo trace," where bison from the Illinois plains had once waded across the river into Kentucky to find salt. The trace, or large animal trail, had also been an Indian trail and, later, a wagon trail. In the twentieth century, it became a highway. Astoundingly, the ground beneath the pavement where we walked in downtown Louisville was once trodden upon by millions of bison. This incredible progression of change has taken just two centuries.

"I like the analogy: first a herd of buffalo and now a herd of humans crossing the river," quipped a walker we had nicknamed "Water" due to his affinity for the precious liquid. "But it makes me sad that this continent may never again see a herd of buffalo come through here. That's what appeals to me about Alaska and Africa—there are still herds of wildlife on the move."

From our camp in a city park beside the Ohio River, we watched its historic waters turn ablaze in sunset glory. A renovated paddleboat churned by, filled with tourists, followed by a giant barge. A nearby port was outlined in lights. Thanks to the Clean Water Act, the river's pollution levels have been reduced. The water actually looked swimmable; and Water, indeed, took advantage of the occasion.

Earlier that day, we had passed a rusted sign along a dilapidated bridge that read "Flicking cigarette butts off the bridge may be dangerous." There was a time, not so long ago, when this river and many others would have caught fire due to pollutants. In fact, some did. Fortunately, our nation has made significant accomplishments in its efforts to address our mammoth environmental problems. For many newly industrializing countries, though, sewage treatment and treatment of chemical wastes are still novel ideas. The sacred Ganges, for example, where millions bathe religiously each day, is dangerously polluted. Environmental clean-up technology has not grown at the same rate in India as have our exported seeds of industrial expansion.

Another responsibility we all share, along with environmental clean-up, is the nurturing of endangered cultures.

In our own country, the native culture is not the only one that has nearly been lost, of course. African Americans, whose ancestors were unwillingly brought here, face a similar challenge.

In Kentucky, near Frankfort, we walkers met a man who is facing that challenge head on—Gregory "Bale" McKnight, a teacher of African culture in the Kentucky school system. Outside a health food store, Gregory opened his car trunk to show us the traditional wood-and-hide drums he had made. "I've been to Africa several times," he said, "learning the ways of my people." He believed that by rediscovering African culture, African Americans could better discover themselves. Through his quest, he had come to realize similarities between the African and many other cultures; thus, he could identify with Native Americans and their purpose. "If I had known you were coming, I would have set up something," he said. Being a man of purpose and pride, he evinced an enthusiasm that was contagious.

Many others along the Kentucky highways were also open and warm, as they shared their knowledge of preserving apples, raising horses, and growing tobacco and fruit trees. It was becoming clear to us that our real power regarding outreach lay, not in mass gatherings, but in these intimate wayside encounters.

"A lot of these roads you're following used to be old buffalo trails," said an old timer in a country store. "The Indians and the pioneers both used them because they were the easiest paths to take, and that's one reason they had so many conflicts. It's not that the pioneers and Indians fought because there were so many of them in the area—there weren't. It's just that they were following the same trails!"

Along the Kanawha River in St. Albans, West Virginia, a Cherokee man named Charlie crossed our path. He was hitchhiking to his cabin twenty miles into the hills. "The Cherokees were on this side of the river," he said. "There are Indian mounds all around here."

An earnest look came across his brown face when he spoke of the land. It was a look I had seen on other faces at the Four Corners and in South Dakota. I had the feeling that Charlie wished the Kanawha Valley were still in Cherokee hands.

"The Cherokees were force-marched to Oklahoma on the Trail of Tears," he continued, "though a band still remains in North Carolina."

As we spoke, traffic rushed by, the sun dipped behind the hills, and a mall's bright lights came on. A barge honked its way up the Kanawha, slicing through ghosts of Cherokee dugouts.

Charlie had built a cabin on land presently owned by the coal company. He hoped for squatter's rights in nine more years. He lived alone, and I felt empathy for him, knowing how hard it is to live out a dream without companionship.

As the days passed and the trees showed signs of fall color, I often thought about Charlie and other native people who were similarly isolated. Images flashed in my mind of the many routes the natives had been forced to take as the government marched them to lands west of the Mississippi. Bear Heart and other contemporary Native Americans I knew had lost ancestors on these marches. I began to envision a future walk through the eastern United States, one that would connect with remnant enclaves of native people and spread healing energy over ground that had absorbed many tears.

Each day, someone thanked me for following through with my inspiration for the Walk for the Earth, but now I knew there were more steps to take; our work was not finished. I often thought of Bear Heart's words to me: "We need to establish a network of love around the world. . . ."

Winding through West Virginia coal country, we took a short cut down a mountain road through a narrow valley known as a "holler" because you could holler across its width. Squeezed into the holler was the town of Mammoth. Houses stood only a few feet from the road. It was easy to talk with residents, since the road abutted their front porches. Few cars or trucks drowned out conversations; this was a quiet holler.

Being at the back of the line of walkers, I was besieged with questions from the curious residents: "Where y'all going? What's this all about? Where ya'll from?" In turn, I asked just as many questions about their area and lives.

"Yep, coal mining is a sick business," summarized one retired miner. "My hand is crumpled up from a machine accident. I got black lung, and the doctors are cleaning coal dust out of my arteries. But I get a good pension, and my medical care is paid for." He said that mining shafts had been tunneled all through the surrounding hills, and that some contained dangerous gases. He had seen shafts collapse on buddies.

Another resident told us a nearby mountain had once been closed off because of poisonous mining gases. Someone else urged us to be on our guard, as we were entering bear country. Then a woman stopped me and said emphatically, "This nuclear thing just has to stop!"

She and I talked for awhile. I told her about problems we had witnessed with uranium mining in the Southwest, problems that struck me as similar to those produced by coal mining. People became sick and the environment polluted. Surface strip-mining was often aesthetically and environmentally devastating; entire mountains were often carved away and stream valleys filled with debris. But deep-shaft mining often took another toll—on the miners. Still, one former miner gazed at the colorful landscape and said adamantly, "I wouldn't take anything for these hills!"

Along the way, a "boy" on a bicycle stopped to talk. He was the size of a nine- or ten-year-old, but his face looked hardened. He chuckled. "It looks like half of you need a haircut!" As we talked, I learned that this "boy" was twenty years old. He was stunted and somewhat retarded from malnutrition and perhaps intermarriage within families, which is a common occurrence in small Appalachian communities.

Soon the number of houses thinned and only mountain peace remained, in its complete fall glory. Goldenrod, aster, staghorn sumac, sycamore, American beech, maple, sassafras—all were blooming or turning color. We feasted on ripe, succulent paw paws. Crystal creeks invited us to cool our feet and rinse our tired bodies. After six-and-a-half months of walking, the Appalachian autumn seemed a just reward.

"Do you ever sit back and look at what you've done, Doug?" a walker named Rosie asked, pointing to our mushrooming group. Our number had risen to more than forty, plus one dog. More were expected. It wasn't the numbers that filled me with pride. It was the obvious transformation of several participants. Many were lighter, happier, wiser.

CHAPTER FOURTEEN

One of my goals for this and for future walks was to uproot people from their everyday lifestyles and prompt them to reexamine their place in the universe. The walking community was a means for this change. If a new consciousness is to emerge, one necessary for the survival and fulfillment of our species, then it must be through community and harmony with the earth.

The end of the walk was looming, but we weren't preoccupied with it; there were too many moments to savor. A Mennonite man, for instance, leading a horse and wearing a black, straight-brimmed hat, greeted us along a Dayton, Virginia highway. As cars and trucks roared by, he told us about the simple lifestyle of the Mennonites and the Amish. We shared a common bond, as we were equally odd to mainstream society—his people used the horse and buggy for transportation, while we walked.

"There are about 150 buggies in this area and 500 Mennonites," he said. "When we drive our buggies, the car drivers are usually very courteous, and, with this new four-lane road, there is more shoulder to ride on. The biggest challenge is in finding a horse that doesn't get skittish when the big trucks pass."

The Mennonite paused. Then, seeing our interest, he continued, "A man up the road still makes carriages, but it's hard to get a good carriage these days because the old hickories have been consumed and not replaced. Some of us have carriages made of fiberglass now. We also put special metal in our horseshoes to make them last longer, so we do use some modern technology."

As the sun dipped over the mountains, we left this gentle man. "Now, you folks have a good day for the rest of this one and for those that follow," he said in parting. We walked on, seeing carriages and horses tied to hitching posts in front of stores and hearing the clomping of horse hooves. The sounds and images stirred something deep inside me; perhaps it was a soul memory.

In contrast, along Highway 42 not long afterward, we passed one of the largest turkey processing plants in the world. Live turkeys were being placed upside down on a conveyor belt, hooked by their feet. A terrible stench of burning feathers permeated the air. As I glimpsed workers dressed in their white plastic outfits, I imagined the emotional detachment they had to maintain. No wonder the Mennonites and Amish chose to evolve more slowly and to raise and process most of their own food.

The remaining days of the walk seemed to whiz by. We trekked a portion of the Appalachian Trail in the Shenandoah Mountains, but our large number—more than fifty, now—made for a noisy hike. New walkers, many of them friends and relatives, showed up daily as we made our way out of the Appalachians and back onto shoulders of busy highways. Places to camp became difficult to find, so we mostly stayed in churches. One was a Baptist Church Center that had harbored Martin Luther King, Jr.'s Poor People's Campaign, a caravan that had included mule trains.

As we entered Washington, D.C., the fast pace of this busy, highly political city affirmed a growing feeling that it might not have been the ideal ending point for the walk. Maybe Plymouth Rock would have been more appropriate, given our purpose. Still, as we crossed the mirror-like Potomac on the Key Bridge, our excitement grew. I felt honored that the group wished for me to carry the staff.

We circled before the White House's big iron gates, sang a song, and posed for a United Press International photo. From across the street, a boy with flowing red hair rushed to us and dove into our outstretched arms. It was our ten-year-old walker Michael! He was the boy who had walked with us from San Francisco to the Four Corners and had read a poem at our sendoff gathering. His father and he had taken a bus from California to join us for the end. Michael looked taller.

At the stern urging of security guards, we left the White House and walked to the Calvary Methodist Church, our home for the next couple of days. In this poor section of D.C., near the political heartbeat of the world's richest nation, burned out tenements, mounds of trash, alcoholics, and homeless people were commonplace. Washington's veil of opulence, the centerpiece being the White House, seemed paper-thin. Inside that church, however, we felt joy and warmth as we shared with each other and with old friends and family members who were arriving for our final gathering.

Our short walk the next morning barely caused a ripple in the national media, nor did it interfere with Washington's day-to-day hubbub. But for our small group, it was momentous. With banners unfurled, we marched from the White House to the Capitol building, joyous and a little sad and anxious now that the walk was ending. Many of us would soon be looking for places to settle and for jobs.

Appropriately, on this last mile, we gave the sacred staff to Joe, our "every stepper," the only one who had walked every step of the way from Point Reyes, California. He protested, saying I should carry it instead, but we insisted.

With head up, Joe's wiry, tanned body walked with the joyful gait we had grown fond of watching. Raven's words from that early sweat ceremony at Point Reyes returned to me: "The weakest among you shall be the strongest." I asked Joe how he felt. In his quiet way, he simply replied, "Proud!"

Proud. That's how most of us felt on that clear, warm afternoon, with seagulls soaring overhead. Those birds reminded me of another day on another coast, when the thirty-five people in our original group had taken a big first step together, hopeful and a little frightened of what America and their inner dragons would show them.

We had persevered seven months of hardships, struggled through differences, and celebrated our diversity. Early on, I thought the first line of young Michael's poem on that first day might be prophetic, "We have lost the secret of the tribe . . ." But in the end, we had found within ourselves what it means to be a tribe of many colors. I felt we would all be stronger for it and contribute to our respective communities after our separation. Whether we would become or continue being teachers, nurses, business owners, farmers, writers, or parents, something of the walk would resonate, inspiring new visions and positive actions. The end was also a beginning. And for me, more walks would follow. I had learned a valuable lesson: Visions can become reality.

Part

THREE

THE TRAIL OF TEARS

Chapter

15

WALK TO THE RISING SUN

T he walk across the United States had been all I had
envisioned and more. A vision is just a glimpse. It
takes an actual experience to complete it. The experience of that walk had helped me to understand
what it means to be part of a community, to take leadership
when necessary, and to step back at other times so that others could have a turn. We touched many people along the
way, through one-on-one contact, small community gatherings, or local and regional media outlets. Would our messages of peace, ecological sanity, and Native American rights
prompt any real social change? That was anyone's guess, but
I had faith that it would, at least on a small scale. The alternative was never to have acted on my vision.

Immediately after the walk, though, I experienced a let-
down. You don't spend seven extraordinary months on the
road, all the way from Point Reyes to Washington, D.C.,
and then simply come home to an eight-to-five job and live

happily ever after. For one thing, my marriage with Julie was ending. The divorce was as amicable as those things go, and we continue to be friends. Walking across the country, she says, "was one of the most amazing things I've ever done."

Some time later, a new woman, Cyndi, walked into my life, eventually quitting her job as office manager for an oil company to join me. By that time, an old canvas teepee a friend gave me had led to an idea: Since I wanted to save money for future walks, why not live in a teepee? With trial and error and help from a wonderful little paperback called *The Indian Tipi: Its History, Construction, and Use*, I erected a Plains Indian–style lodge in the heart of north Florida's piney woods. It leaked, but it was economical.

One morning an unusual occurrence distracted Cyndi and me: We saw a toddler-sized spirit child gleefully running around the teepee. We were dumbfounded. When the waking vision faded, we simultaneously asked each other, "Did you see that?" It seemed clear that a new life was seeking to join ours. So, with our monetary circumstances questionable at best, we put our faith in a Higher Power. Everything would work out. In fact, I already knew the name of our future child—Cheyenne—in honor of the people from whom I had learned so many lessons.

And so it was with full hearts that, several months later, in 1986 we set out on the Trail of Tears Walk, my inspiration for which had come about in a vision during the previous walk across the United States. In the vision, I had seen different groups of Native Americans being forced to march from their southeastern homelands to Oklahoma Territory, many hundreds of miles away.

Conceived by Thomas Jefferson during his presidency and carried out by Andrew Jackson in the 1830s, the United States government had forcibly moved tens of thousands of Cherokee, Creek, Choctaw, Chickasaw, and Seminole from their homelands to Oklahoma Territory. Their many relocation routes resembled a spider's web across the Southeast. The rationale was that white settlers used the land more productively than Indians and that removal would protect the Indians from white predation. In reality, it was a blatant land grab.

It is difficult to determine how many people perished on what was to be known as "The Trail Where They Cried," or "The Trail of Tears," but the Cherokee alone lost more than four thousand. And once the survivors reached present-day Oklahoma, they suffered from hunger and psychological shock, and many died of epidemic diseases. It was, in my view, one of the darkest periods of American history, and its repercussions are still being felt.

When I had first envisioned a walk that encompassed many routes of the Trail of Tears, I had wondered why the images of the exiled Native Americans were coming to me. The wind itself seemed to be giving me the answer: "Walk with a prayerful attitude, and heal some of their descendants' pain." It also became clear that the walk should be from west to east to represent a symbolic return to the ancestral homelands, east being the direction of new beginnings, according to most Native American traditions. We would seek to connect with as many of the different relocated tribes as possible on this journey that we hoped would be spiritually healing for others as well as for ourselves.

The starting point I had chosen for the walk was Fountainhead State Park, Oklahoma. It being late February and extremely cold and windy, the park was deserted. I wondered why it was even open, unless it was to lure unsuspecting Floridians to camp there. The walk was to begin on March 1. We had arrived two days early to go over logistics, but I questioned the wisdom of having come at all.

Cyndi, especially, was uncomfortable. Now seven months pregnant, she was finding it difficult to sleep with any ease, much less in a tent on the hard ground. She was good-natured about the predicament, though, as she usually was about such things.

The Trail of Tears Walk I had envisioned was to be twelve-hundred miles long, from its inception at Fountainhead Park to its end point at Rattlesnake Springs, Tennessee, one of the embarking points for the Cherokee Trail of Tears. I had planned a horseshoe-shaped route that would cover the ancestral lands of the Choctaw, Chickasaw, Muskogee, Seminole, and Cherokee peoples, commonly referred to as the Five Civilized Tribes. Averaging fifteen miles a day, with a day off every week, we planned to take more than four months for the journey.

Not expecting a big crowd for the walk, I was nevertheless mindful of the many letters we had received in its support, several of them from Native Americans. Some expressed concern over the thousands of Navajo Indians who currently faced removal at Big Mountain, their plight seeming to run parallel to what had occurred in the Southeast in the early 1800s. And so we incorporated their cause into our walk.

At the park three veteran walkers joined us: Rosie, Debbie, and John, the man who had won the colt on the

Pine Ridge Reservation. Rosie had also been on that trip, and she and Debbie had participated in a subsequent walk I had led in Europe. Both women were from balmy Miami. Lively and caring, they loved being around people and being of service to others.

Hailing from Winters, California, John was their complement—quiet, mellow, and clear in his sense of purpose. If no one else had shown up, John would have walked the route alone. I had grown to expect that kind of dedication from the man who had won a beautiful horse and then immediately given it away.

Around six o'clock on the first evening we were all together, wind, darkness, and cold drove us into our tents. I tried to read by candlelight, but I was distracted with worry about the weather and the baby and how people would receive us. This was crazy, I told myself—five people huddled in the inclement Oklahoma woods to fulfill a vision. Who cared? But if I was in danger of losing faith, Cyndi never did. Despite her discomfort, she didn't question our purpose or my sanity, and I loved her for it.

The day before our planned embarkation, we took a field trip to view the fabulous art of transplanted southeastern Native Americans exhibited at the Five Civilized Tribes Museum in Muscogee. "I am honored you are here," a Cherokee cashier at the museum remarked. "You must tell our newspaper in Muscogee what you are doing. People need to know."

During the ensuing interview with a journalist, we tried to explain why five warm-climate people were camped in an abandoned state park, about to embark on a four-month journey through cold, rain, heat, poison ivy, bugs, rednecks, snakes. . . . We stepped outside to shiver for a photograph and then returned to camp to make a fire, the winds finally calming. A stray black dog and her puppy soon befriended us, followed by two women from the Creek Indian tribal government. The women had come to interview us for the tribal newspaper, but we mostly joked, talked, built the fire higher, and filled our coffee mugs.

"I read your first newsletter about the Great Spirit speaking to you through the wind to organize the walk," said one of the women, "and something clicked. Since then the wind has been speaking to me. I'm trying to learn more about my heritage."

We wondered aloud if the Indian ways were largely being lost or whether they were reemerging. We concluded that both were happening. Adaptation, perseverance, and innovation are the tenets of any culture that survives.

The next morning, March 1, we finally prepared to leave. Our two Creek friends returned to send us off. So did the mother dog and pup. The ranger said he would destroy the dogs if we didn't take them, so what choice did we have? Their cold noses, playful wrestling, and games of tug-of-war with sticks proved to be good ways to forget the sore muscles at the end of that long first day.

After the third day of walking, muscular soreness had really set in, but receiving free pie and coffee at Don's Café in Stigler, Oklahoma, helped. "My great-grandmother walked that Trail of Tears," said one waitress. "She's buried up on the hill."

Near a landing where groups of Cherokee and Choctaw had been dropped off from a riverboat on their respective Trails of Tears, we camped in an oak grove along the Arkansas

River. Many of the reluctant immigrants had settled into the region, at that time simply called "Indian Territory." Within a century, they had lost most of their land to white settlers, especially during the movement toward Oklahoma statehood in 1907 and then during the Great Depression. Ironically, some Indians had to serve as tenant farmers on their own former terrain, since they had nowhere else to go. Presently, a few tribes are buying back land and trying to remedy the high unemployment rate that plagues Indian people in some Oklahoma counties.

We visited the nearby Spiro Mound State Archeological Site, which had been a major East-West trade center a thousand years ago. There, flint, crystals, engraved shells, copper, carved effigy pipes, and other objects had been bartered. Traders had traveled by canoe and on foot along a vast trade network that extended to Illinois, Florida, the East Coast, and parts of the West. We could only imagine the adventures that had once occurred on those journeys.

Near Sallisaw, we also visited the cabin and shrine of the Cherokee known as Sequoyah. Before removal from his native Tennessee, Sequoyah had labored for nearly two decades to develop a Cherokee alphabet, often writing on slabs of wood and bark. In 1821, the Cherokee Nation officially adopted Sequoyah's alphabet. Within months, most Cherokees had learned how to read and write it. Sequoyah is believed to be the only human being in history to develop an entire alphabet on his own.

Continuing the walk the next day, we met a mother and her two young daughters at a convenience store. They fell in love with our furry companions, even though the dogs still reeked of skunk from an encounter two nights before. It had taken several cans of tomato juice and hot water to wash off the worst of it. After a warm interaction, Rosie made the pitch: "They're yours if you can provide them a good home."

The mother was ecstatic. "This is amazing," she said. "I've been wanting two black dogs." The family lived on fifteen acres of land; we knew the dogs would be happy. Our canine friends hopped into their car, the two girls squealing over the cute puppy. They never looked back.

We missed our companions, but we wondered if losing them was somehow symbolic, given the nature of our odyssey. Perhaps southeastern native people, on their journey to Oklahoma, had left pets with sympathetic settlers along the way to spare them the harsh rigors of a forced march—one that produced thousands of unmarked graves. Certainly, they had left *human* loved ones behind, especially those who had hidden or intermarried with white or black people. As a consequence, now native people of the same tribe are often separated by more than a thousand miles. Only in recent years has the communication rift been bridged.

Compared to the original people on the various Trails of Tears, we, of course, had luxuries that made the trip bearable. For one, we had an automobile—Rosie's car—as a support vehicle. The full significance of that advantage became clear one night when a man awakened us at the Viking Village Campground in Arkansas. "A big storm's coming," he said. "Supposed to have hail and high winds."

Soon after he left, a gust blew over Cyndi's and my tent, with us in it! Soaking wet, she and I retreated to the car and sat inside shivering as we watched rain pelt the windshield.

But we, at least, were out of the downpour, unlike the original walkers on the Trails of Tears would have been.

Despite extremes of weather, we trekked through rural Arkansas, enjoying peaceful mountains and rushing rivers. Cyndi could have driven the support vehicle the entire time, but she insisted on walking several miles a day. With her thin frame and watermelon-sized belly, she was a sight to behold along the rural highways. "I feel as if I'm carrying a backpack in front of me," she joked to a newspaper reporter.

To help pass time and earn extra money, John began collecting returnable pop bottles. He was always surprised at the large number he would find, as well as thankful that throwaways hadn't completely taken over Arkansas' soft-drink market.

On April Fools Day, we crossed the mighty Mississippi River on the Greenville Bridge near the spot where southeastern native people had been loaded onto ferries to continue their relocation west. Bear Heart, in his book *The Wind Is My Mother*, describes the ordeal his people endured crossing the Mississippi, what they called the *We-o-gof-ke*:

> I knew a man who went on that long walk as a child and he told me about it. At one point the people and the few horses they had were put on twelve dilapidated ferry-boats to cross the Mississippi River. The ferry started sinking, so he grabbed his little sister, got on a horse, and headed for shore, all the while chased by soldiers who didn't want him riding. He was trying to hurry but the horse had to swim and was frightened from the commotion, so it was slow going. He had seen how

brutal the soldiers could be and how the ferries were intentionally overloaded to make them sink, so he was making a break for his life. . . . Many of our people died crossing the Mississippi. When the survivors got across the river, many were soaked from swimming and it was freezing cold.[1]

Bear Heart goes on to point out that, even with the sad background of the Trail of Tears, Indian boarding schools, and the like, "Today in our ceremonies, many of our people still pray for all mankind, whether they be black, yellow, red, or white."[2] While the past is not often forgotten, lest it be repeated, many native people have embraced the highest attributes of universal love.

Entering Mississippi, we felt the heat bear down on us as we passed Indian temple mounds near Greenville, remnants of a ceremonial complex that once extended throughout the Southeast and Midwest and thrived between twelve hundred and five hundred years ago.

On a windy, blue-sky day, walking along a rural highway, I could easily envision early mounds and villages, along with virgin forests, where there were now fields and towns, and foot trails where asphalt highways now cut through the land. The native people, having lived there for millennia, had made a strong psychic imprint. Many natives believe that the soul of the land—as it existed before pollution and massive environmental destruction—is still alive, and that early people and all those who now strive to live in harmony with the earth are part of it. One can feel and even see it at times and know it as true—just one more mystery to contemplate.

More recent events have also left a lasting imprint on the Mississippi landscape. The civil rights movement exposed the dark heart of racism. We were honored to walk part of the path of the Meredith Mississippi Freedom March, which in 1966 had been led by Dr. Martin Luther King, Jr. and Stokely Carmichael. They were continuing the solo walk of James Meredith's "March against Fear." Meredith had planned the walk to be 220 miles long, but he had been shot by a white racist on the second day of his trek. King explained his reason for taking up the cause in his autobiography: "Meredith began his lonely journey as a pilgrimage against fear. Wouldn't failure to continue only intensify the fears of the oppressed and deprived Negroes of Mississippi? Would this not be a setback for the whole civil rights movement and a blow to nonviolent discipline?"[3] Fortunately, Meredith would recover enough from his wound to join the walk near its conclusion.

One evening, in the town of Canton, we stayed at the Holy Child Jesus Church Convent and school that had sheltered King and his marchers from angry mobs and the police. Perusing church scrapbooks, we were struck by the irony of how both sides justified their positions by quoting biblical passages.

At the time of our visit, the population of Canton was 80 percent African-American, although several sections of the town were excluded from the city limits to weigh voting in favor of the whites. Most white children attended a private academy, while blacks attended public or Catholic elementary schools, even though most are not Catholic.

The morning after we arrived, Debbie got a taste of racism firsthand. She was in a convenience store where a black man bought fifty crickets for $3.50. A white man followed and bought the same number of crickets for a dollar. When Debbie pointed out the discrepancy to the shopkeeper, he glared at her as if she had violated an unspoken law. It was the same type of discrimination that still often besets Native Americans.

After a windy walk, we stayed in the town of Camden at the house of Sister Mary Grace, or "Mama," as she was called. She was a leader in the war on poverty and racism, earning the trust of whites and blacks alike.

"It will take a couple more generations to turn things around more completely here," she said, "but it is happening." Her key to success was peaceful loving action, not labeling people as racist or bigoted. "I know one store owner who calls himself a racist and a bigot, but because of the way I am approaching him, he is helping us out immensely."

After our visit with "Mama," Cyndi and I returned home to await the birth of our child. Rosie, Debbie, and John carried on the walk, visiting and touring the Choctaw Reservation in the town of Philadelphia, Mississippi, and the Poarch Creek Reservation near Atmore, Alabama. With government assistance, Indian people in those areas have risen from the depths of poverty to organize economically viable communities.

In one small town, the three remaining walkers were allowed to camp overnight near a county fair. They enjoyed the fair until they met a local police officer. "He was a big guy—pot belly, big gun, and a hard stare—the kind of cop that you wouldn't want to mess with," Rosie recalled. "He knew who we were and why we were there. He said to us, 'You take a nigger and put him in a $500 suit with a $100 briefcase and $100 shoes, and you know what you get? A nigger.'

"None of us challenged him. You knew that he had grown up that way, and that he was probably was trying to get a rise out of us, but I felt a small part of what it must be like to be on the receiving end of prejudice, whether you are black, Native American, or anyone else who isn't white-Christian-American born. It felt terrible and very scary."

Overall, Rosie enjoyed the daily life of a walk, even if with a smaller group than had gone on the two previous ones. "We became so used to the walking that the body just went by itself," she said, "one foot after the other until you reached a rhythm that allowed your mind to fly free and create visions and clarity. We called it a moving meditation."

She went on, "My little yellow Toyota was the carry-all for most of this walk, which meant that someone had to leapfrog the car ahead; we took turns driving about four miles at a time. So, even if we covered twenty miles a day, we weren't as tired as we had been on the other walks. We had the energy in the evenings for visiting a café, playing backgammon, and talking with the locals. We tried to let people know why we were walking, in order to make up for not having the larger public gatherings we had had on our first walk.

"In these conversations, it was easy to point out the difference between the trek we were making by choice and the one the Native Americans were compelled to make on the Trail of Tears. We tried to imagine being forced to walk day after day to a strange place with no support or purpose or anything resembling a creature comfort."

In west Florida, the walkers passed dark rivers with stark, white sand banks, rolling hills covered with longleaf and sand pine, and flowering pitcher-plant bogs. They walked through the sprawling Eglin Air Force Base, "sowing the seeds of peace," according to John. "The walk was so much larger than the relatively small number of us," he concluded. "It was important for me to help mend the broken hoop."

John reflected a feeling many of us shared. The southeastern Native American people had been persecuted for centuries and nearly decimated—with their power, or "hoop," broken. We hoped that any attempt we made to support their recovery, even symbolically through a walk, would help.

Still awaiting the birth of our baby, Cyndi and I rejoined the walkers in the North Florida Creek town of Bruce. Having been a member of nearby Creek Indian ceremonial grounds for several years, I knew many of the people; they received us warmly with a huge potluck dinner. The Creek descendants had established a center in an old schoolhouse, one that also served as headquarters for the Muscogee Nation of Florida. Paintings and photos of early native people lined the walls. Some were dark-skinned ancestors of residents. Many modern Florida Creeks, however, do not look racially Indian due to generations of intermarriage with European descendants and sometimes African-Americans.

I had originally come to know the Creeks in a most unusual manner. Three years earlier, I had attended a New Year's Eve dance at a local cooperative community near Miccosukee, Florida. At the end of the evening, I was walking through a meadow to my car soon after midnight. Frost blanketed the ground; a million tiny particles sparkled in the moonlight as if to reflect the panorama of stars above. My breath in the crisp air formed momentary clouds.

That's when Aunt Alice first appeared.

She was a bluish, semi-transparent figure standing on the illuminated ground. She said nothing, did nothing, but I felt a sudden connection to my surroundings. She seemed part of the air, the grass, and the very ground beneath my feet. Sensing that she was Native American, I was not afraid.

Growing up, I had been no stranger to spirit visitors, but my reaction wasn't always calm. When I was four, my baby rattle rose up from my crib and shook in midair, then dropped. I screamed until my parents came. When I was twelve, my grandmother visited me a year after she had died. She tried to say something, but it came out garbled. I slept in my parent's bed for several nights afterward.

Then when I had met Bear Heart, he had helped me overcome my fear of such experiences. Under his tutelage, visitations by ancestors, animal spirits, and the "little people" were not exactly commonplace, but they began to feel like a part of the natural flow of life. The more connected I felt to Mother Earth, the less uncomfortable I was. So seeing this Native American spirit woman on New Year's Eve had not been frightening—it was just perplexing. If only I could understand the purpose of her visit!

In the following weeks, my mysterious visitor had often revealed herself to me, always in nature. Her visitations occurred at times when I felt particularly attuned to my surroundings, and her presence seemed to accentuate the feeling. With each visit, my sense grew that she wanted me to do something. She was extending some sort of invitation, but to where?

That March, I had visited a small museum south of Tallahassee featuring the area's Muskogee Creek Indian culture and history. In talking with the museum curator, I soon gathered that this fair-skinned man also served as a spiritual leader for a small group of mixed-blood Creeks who still carried on their ancient ceremonial ways. I felt moved to describe the spirit woman to this elder.

When I did so, he pulled out a copy of a painting. The subject was an elderly Indian woman who bore a Mona Lisa smile. She wore an old coat. A shawl covered her head. The artist portrayed her feet and walking stick as part of the earth beneath her and of the live oak next to which she was standing.

"That's what the artist saw when he painted her," said the elder. I stared at the painting, transfixed by the woman's deep eyes and soft, reflective face.

"Is this the woman?" he asked.

"Why yes—yes it is!" I said, startled.

"That's Aunt Alice. She passed away a couple years ago."

I felt tingly all over, and somehow pure and childlike, elated at finally being able to identify my mysterious visitor.

"It seems that she wants me to go somewhere," I said.

The elder began talking about the Creek ceremonial grounds a few miles away. Known as a "square grounds" and often called "the grounds," it featured brush-covered sitting platforms or arbors placed in each of the cardinal direction points around a sacred fire mound.

During ceremonies, the sacred fire was lit only after the grounds had been cleared of weeds, raked, and swept and a fresh topping of willow branches had been placed on each of the brush arbors. A circular ring of shells surrounded the cleared area, marking the separation between the secular and the sacred worlds just as they do between land and water along a shoreline.

Before participating in events at the grounds, the people purified themselves by fasting and sometimes by joining in a sweat lodge ceremony. The idea was to create a clean place for the One Above to sit among the people. The fire was considered a piece of the life-giving sun and a vessel through which the Maker of Breath could communicate, similar to the burning bush of the Old Testament. As a show of respect, no trash was ever thrown into the fire, and participants tried not to walk between another person and the fire or to cast a shadow on it, so as not to interrupt an interaction that might have been occurring.

After a ceremony, the sacred fire would be carried in portable oil lamps from the grounds to various participants' homes. There, as part of a relatively modern innovation, it was kept burning in the form of gas pilot lights until it was time to carry it back to the grounds again for the next occasion. The fire was only allowed to go out just prior to the lighting of the new fire at the annual Green Corn Ceremony early each summer.

At different times of year, the sacred fire was present for dances, baby blessings, weddings, and naming ceremonies. People prayed around the fire, revealing their innermost hopes and fears. People brought forth their troubles in hopes the flames would consume them. People expressed their deepest love and appreciation, and they always offered tobacco to the flames as native people have done for millennia. The subsequent smoke was a visible reminder of their prayers rising toward the Upper World.

The elder at the museum explained that the group's size had fluctuated significantly over past decades as a result of removals, persecution, disease, wars, and missionary pressure. He went on to say that the woman in the painting had grown up attending a Creek ceremonial grounds in Alabama. It had eventually disbanded, and so when she moved to Florida and found the nearby ceremonial "square grounds" in the late 1960s, she was ecstatic. She became a respected elder of the grounds and was affectionately called Aunt Alice by all who knew her. In the early 1970s, she was especially helpful in guiding a huge influx of newcomers who had been spurred by two simultaneous events: a government docket releasing money to eastern Creek descendants and the popularization of Indian culture by movies and books. People had wild ideas about what being Indian was about. Aunt Alice set them straight.

In relating to the outside world, Aunt Alice was discreet about her knowledge of and participation at the grounds, partly because many in her family were evangelical Christians who labeled traditional Indian gatherings as "devil worship." She, as did many elders, also remembered stories told by parents and grandparents of persecution, when being Indian could mean death or being sent to a far-off land known today as Oklahoma.

"She acted in quiet ways, with no pretenses," said the elder. "Once, she even cured a child who had tuberculosis by boiling up pine sap into a medicinal salve and rubbing it over the chest area." He paused and looked at me thoughtfully. He seemed to be listening to an inner voice. "I think

Aunt Alice wants you to visit the grounds," he concluded. I nodded in agreement. Aunt Alice's purpose was finally revealed.

Later, I was to learn about the Creek motto: "The Fire chooses its own." The Creeks have a cultural bias against proselytizing, and everyone I've talked with has a different story about how they came to the grounds. Generally, it was as if invisible threads had pulled them there. I myself could thank one of its gatekeepers, Aunt Alice.

Soon after the gathering in Bruce, the walkers headed east toward these same ceremonial grounds, which had once been adjacent to a Creek reservation before the majority of natives were relocated. As we approached the circle of shells, we felt honored that many Creeks had gathered to welcome us. We heard their laughter and excited voices in the kitchen area and in the large community "chickee," a traditional open-sided structure roofed with palm branches. The sound warmed my heart. As Bear Heart used to say, "Indians aren't moping about the buffalo all the time. We like to laugh, tell jokes." People at the grounds often find humor in life, especially when they gather together. And laughter is good medicine.

After introductions and greetings, I crossed the shell ring, quietly approaching the sacred fire that burned bright on its knee-high mound. I greeted the fire like an old friend, offering tobacco. At a later date, we would have the Green Corn Ceremony, an observance that involves releasing the old year and beginning a new one. The "busk," as it is called, includes fasting, ceremonial dances, herbal medicines, lively stickball games, and a grand feast.

As did traditional Creeks, I had come to view the sacred fire as a spiritual conduit and transport through time. The fire connects one to grounds of long ago, to villages and people no longer seen in the physical world, and to future generations. I made a silent prayer for the walk, for the Creek people, and for the successful birth of Cyndi's and my child.

Soon my prayer seemed to be answered: Five days later, with a Creek Indian flint blade, I cut the umbilical cord of my daughter, Cheyenne Jean Hunt-Alderson, minutes after her birth at four o'clock in the morning at a Tallahassee hospital. To see my daughter's head emerge from the womb and take her first gasps of air brought many tears.

By good fortune, Cheyenne's birth coincided with the walkers' arrival in Tallahassee. The group had temporarily grown to twelve for a small Walk-for-the-Earth reunion, and they held a vigil for us at a nearby lake. For those of us who had undertaken a walk to honor the incredible ordeal of the Native Americans' Trail of Tears, Cheyenne's birth was a joyful reminder that new life can emerge from the ashes.

Chapter

16

CHEROKEE LANDS

yndi and I soon rejoined the Trail of Tears walk with our newborn daughter in north Georgia. In addition, an elder had joined the group—Katherine Stanley of Tallahassee, a member of the Western Cherokee Tribe of Oklahoma. With Katherine and the baby, we now had three generations on the walk, which gave it an extended-family feeling.

While we had been away, the walkers had suffered through a south Georgia heat wave. John pointed to the sweat stains on his journal acquired from hiking through the "heat-searing mugginess." He also told a story about the first day that another new walker, Elladon, had joined the group. Elladon was a great fan of science fiction who somehow looked the part with his long brown hair and glasses.

"Elladon is a middle-earth troll," began John. "When we stopped for a break, he fell asleep in midsentence sitting against a tree. . . ." The Deep South summer, combined with rigorous exercise, can be a shock to any unsuspecting northerner—be he from middle earth or beyond.

Fortunately, for the sake of our baby and new elder, as well as for Elladon, north Georgia was forested and hilly, and a few blessed degrees cooler as a result. This was Cherokee country. We camped beside the house of a kind white family whose ancestors had been there since the Cherokee occupation. Katherine looked at the old photos on the walls. "Those sure were hard-working people," she said. "You can tell by their faces."

"That sounds odd coming from a Cherokee, because those folks of ours kicked the Cherokee off this land," said our hostess. Katherine just nodded. She showed no animosity toward our host family, and they showed none toward her or our purpose. To the contrary, they cooked us a great dinner. Nor was there animosity toward Eric, a twenty-year-old African-American from Ohio. He had slept in a nearby Rome, Georgia, cemetery for three days before finding the walk group at our mail pick-up.

"A few days ago, I wouldn't have dreamed of sitting on this porch in Georgia and playing this man's guitar," Eric said, a look of wonderment in his eyes, "but here I am. And I've never seen a sunset in the mountains until now. That's something I've always wanted to do."

Another new arrival, Anthony, had hitchhiked for a solid week from Seattle. He said he had been afraid of coming to Georgia until a Lakota man had picked him up and told him that, on a long journey the man himself had made, he had met people with good hearts no matter what their race or place of origin. "That really helped," said Anthony. "And I have met some great people."

Water, a veteran of the first walk, joined us, too. He carried a blow-up earth balloon to relay the concept that we are all citizens of the earth and to show people where we had come from and where we were headed.

In gaining new walkers, we lost Rosie and Debbie. They had pressing business in Miami and now felt free to leave, given that we had a new support vehicle in Katherine's van. Since I had been preoccupied with Cheyenne's birth and care, their efforts in my absence had been greatly appreciated.

We walkers had to exercise tolerance and patience as we carefully squeezed us all—plus a baby and our gear—into Katherine's van for a side trip to tourist-oriented Cherokee, North Carolina. We were attending the third grand council of the eastern and western bands of the Cherokee Nation, at which delegates from Oklahoma and North Carolina were meeting to explore their common roots and interests. Upon our arrival, Katherine proudly introduced the walk and each of its participants to the gathering. Many doors opened as a result, and Cheyenne was a big hit.

To end the meeting, the two chiefs, Wilma Mankiller of the Western Cherokee and Robert Youngdeer of the Eastern Cherokee, smoked a huge, two-stemmed pipe representing the two factions. Mankiller, the first elected woman chief of the Cherokee, expressed trepidation about smoking the pipe in front of photographers, a television camera, and an audience. "When we smoke the pipe in Oklahoma," she said, "we do it in private." She made a similar statement when several Eastern Cherokee performed what they described as a ceremonial dance. Her reservations about public display pointed to the differences between the eastern and the western bands.

Afterward, we were impressed by a lively Cherokee stickball game, marked by wrestling and physical contact. Native games such as stickball may have inspired some of our modern sports. Indeed, elements of soccer and football were apparent as the two teams chased a small leather ball with pairs of oak or hickory sticks with webbed ends. Points were made by throwing the ball through a goal on either end of a field. The person who held the ball could be tackled, but there was no rule against tackling a person who *didn't* have the ball, either.

Most southeastern tribes play this Cherokee-style of stickball, but I am more accustomed to the one-pole game played by the Creeks and Seminoles. Also called the "social game," males and females play each other, the boys and men using webbed sticks while the girls and women freely use their hands. The aim is to hit a tall pole with the ball, either at a point above a red line or on a wooden fish or animal skull atop the pole. The game is a lively form of controlled aggression, although accusations of foul play seem to be part of the ritual. Children are often given free shots, partly to make up for their getting run over or jostled about. Sometimes, I've seen games end in a tie just to keep harmony in the camp.

Ceremonies and medicine were traditionally associated with stickball match games, but this element has largely been lost in the East. After the Cherokee demonstration game, one player told us that, in the old days, players would fast and pray all night prior to a game, as part of serious spiritual preparation. "Now, we party!" he said with a smile.

The challenge of visiting a town like Cherokee is in seeing beyond the blatant tourist traps that assault the senses and promote a Hollywood Indian image. Most visitors who seek a strong spiritual connection are frustrated. The town largely portrays what they think the public wants to see— Indians in headdresses and shops selling beads and moccasins. Depth can be difficult to perceive.

Blame the Trail of Tears.

Nevertheless, some elements of the authentic Cherokee culture remain. When the bulk of the Cherokee Nation was relocated to Oklahoma, ceremonial leaders took the sacred fire with them. In 1951, after the passage of almost 120 years, a Cherokee delegation brought a flame from that same fire back to North Carolina! Even though many traditional ways in the East had been lost in the interim, the Western Cherokee had preserved their nation's original sacred fire the entire time. The eternal flame from the 1951 journey now burns behind a glass wall in the town amphitheater where the Cherokee drama "Unto These Hills" is shown.

What also survives in Cherokee, chiefly among elders, is the language, so rich in cultural nuances, as are most indigenous tongues. And a few people still practice ancient herbology and healing ways, along with traditional crafts such as basket making. As is true regarding many indigenous groups, for an outsider to learn these skills depends upon connections and prolonged contact. The same is true about gaining access to the traditional ceremonial grounds that have been revived since the walk, where a group of Eastern Cherokee once again fast, pray, and dance around a sacred fire in a more private setting.

The Cherokee originally survived in the East by hiding from armed soldiers in remote caves and mountain coves.

Understandably, certain aspects of their culture are closely guarded.

Marion Dunn is a Cherokee keeper of stories and myths. She joined us for a gathering of one hundred or so members of the Tennessee Scenic Rivers Association. The focus was on the Cherokee people and on taking care of the earth. In an outdoor amphitheater beside the rushing Hiwassee River, against a backdrop of the smoky blue mountains, Marion gave an inspiring account of Cherokee life, history, and experience on the Trail of Tears. "The white man too often wants more and more," she concluded, "but the Indian way is to enjoy life, to be happy."

I spoke of our walk, contrasting it with the original Trail of Tears. I put forth that many people who were concerned about the environment could deepen their spiritual awareness and understanding through nature and native ways. Dances and ceremonies reflect many aspects of the natural world.

Matt Pritchard, a Cherokee who worked for the Tennessee Conservation Department, said it was inspiring to meet people who were thinking and feeling as Indians do. "That is more important than *looking* Indian," he said. "It is easy to get caught up in making money."

The energy at the gathering seemed to build. When Cyndi and I retired to our tent that night, I felt a strong force beaming from my umbilical region. Closing my eyes, I saw Indian men and women dancing a huge, southern-style friendship dance through the sky. Holding hands, I joined them and soon came to a mountaintop where there was a ring of boulders, as there is at Stonehenge. A light shone in the center. Intuitively, I knew this was the nest of a giant eagle of many colors. My own light and awareness grew in its presence. Soon, the evening's meeting at the amphitheater came into clear view, but now from the perspective of the outside looking in.

Then it hit me! This was the event I had foreseen more than ten years ago on the Appalachian Trail, when, in a vision, I had spoken before a group of good-hearted people with blue mountains in the background. At that time, I had had a strong sense of a spiritual unity, of Native American presence, and of ecological purpose, these elements all being deeply intertwined.

Now, I realized, it was that vision that had pointed the way toward my involvement with the walks, the ecological movement, and the native peoples. What had begun as a flash of inspiration was being fulfilled. I could only give my humblest prayer of thanks. Each preceding step and challenge had opened the way for the next. I was on the right path.

That night, I lay awake for a long time, marveling at the magic of it all.

In approaching the sacred Cherokee grounds of Red Clay, where the Cherokee held their last councils before the Trail of Tears, Katherine insisted on walking the last leg alone, "to get a better feel for what it was like." Some of her ancestors had been on the Trail. She was fulfilling a vision of her own by coming to Red Clay, the site being a type of pilgrimage stop for many Cherokee people. The setting of hills, trees, and reconstructed log cabins evoked a serene feeling.

In the center of the grounds was Council Springs, a clear azure pool that formed a creek. Early council members had taken their traditional seven morning dips in the cool waters, believing that such natural openings in the earth led to another world.

A short distance away, a state museum depicted the dramatic struggle that had occurred in the early 1830s. Soon after President Andrew Jackson had pushed his Indian Removal Act through Congress, the state of Georgia outlawed any Cherokee gathering that was not for removal purposes. Cherokees were stripped of their legal rights, including the right to own land. Thus, the door was swung open for rampant land grabbing and physical abuses.

Being just inside Tennessee, Red Clay had been an ideal meeting ground for the Cherokee. There, delegates from various tribal branches could discuss their common fate without fear of Georgia militias. Hence, it was from Red Clay that Chief John Ross and his compatriots had launched their last desperate attempts to keep their homelands. They won a Supreme Court battle, but President Jackson refused to recognize it. "John Marshall has made his law, now let him enforce it," was Jackson's defiant quote.

In the end, more than sixteen thousand Cherokee were dragged from their homes, some barefoot with few clothes or belongings, and herded into stockades. In the ensuing fourteen-hundred-mile journey west, with only 645 wagons and eight cents a day to feed each person, more than one quarter of the Cherokee Nation died along the way. Only a few escaped, the largest band having hidden in the North Carolina mountains. A sympathetic white settler bought land for the Cherokee to live on in North Carolina, and those who did eventually formed the Eastern Cherokee Reservation, commonly called the Qualla Boundary.

Appropriately, it was at Red Clay in 1984 that twenty thousand Eastern and Western Cherokees were reunited after nearly 150 years. For two days, they were of one tribe, one heart, one mind. They cried with each other, met in council, reaffirmed their common heritage, and planned for the future. In accordance with the belief that more than one sacred fire can burn at the same time as long as they share a common origin, runners lit a torch from the eternal flame in Cherokee and brought it to a glass-enclosed stone altar at Red Clay. There, a gas-fed fire was ignited that burns to this day.

"Electrifying," "sacred," "unity being born." These were some of the words used to describe the Red Clay reunion of 1984. A theme was coined: "Hold fast to the center, preserve the good, and the grievous can be made well." The Red Clay gathering, after so many years of persecution and separation, would have given hope to any oppressed people.

Our being allowed to camp at Red Clay for three days was a privilege, since public camping was normally not allowed. We spent the time talking with the many people we met and hiking through the woods. The rangers were friendly and sensitive to the area. "This place is special," said one of them, named Tom. "You can't help but feel it if you walk between the springs and the sacred fire around sunset."

On the second evening of our visit, the eternal flame in the stone altar went out. Concerned, we rushed to tell Tom. "Damn!" he said, "Not again! The last time that happened, someone had stuffed hamburger in the air vents."

To be true to tradition, the fire would have to be relit from the sacred fire burning in the town of Cherokee —

assuming that that flame had never been extinguished. But this fire was more of a symbolic reminder of the sacred Cherokee fires of the past, and, obviously, not all visitors understood its significance. Without formality, Tom relit it using a wooden match.

When we left Red Clay, several new people joined us for the walk's last stretch, including an Apache man and several people of Cherokee descent. One Eagle, a Cherokee elder, was our guide. A former truck driver, he had a booming voice and hearty sense of humor that made us all feel good. He did a blessing by the spring and encouraged everyone to drink from his hand-carved wooden dipper.

Inspired, we walked to Cleveland, Tennessee, under a hot sun and stopped at a Fourth of July barbecue where One Eagle treated us all to lunch. It seemed odd for a Native American to be participating in an Independence Day celebration. Regarding the native peoples, the United States government's policies had once been so extreme that they had even inspired Adolf Hitler's concept of genocide. We are told that Hitler "often praised to his inner circle the efficiency of America's extermination—by starvation and uneven combat—of the red savages who could not be tamed by captivity."[1] Nevertheless, on this walk as well as the last one across the country, we had found most Native Americans to be patriotic. Perhaps they realized that countries, like people, could evolve, as long as history's lessons are heeded.

After lunch, we shuttled ahead to camp at Rattlesnake Springs, where, in 1838, the majority of Cherokee—over thirteen thousand—had been herded into stockades to await removal to Oklahoma. It was considered the official embarking point of the Cherokee Trail of Tears. An old farmhouse half covered the small springs that gave the place its name.

To the average passerby, Rattlesnake Springs is a quaint dairy farm surrounded by rolling hills. Hidden from view are hundreds of unmarked Cherokee graves. Many had become sick and died in the stockade's horrid conditions. Like the Wounded Knee massacre, the event was never covered in my school history books.

By the time the Native Americans were removed, perhaps no other tribe had assimilated into the encroaching European culture as fully as the Cherokee. Some mixed-blood Cherokee had integrated so successfully into white culture that they were able to build and own large plantations worked by African slaves. A large warrior contingent had helped Andrew Jackson fight hostile Creek Indians during the Red Stick War of the early 1800s. Yet eventually the Cherokee experienced the same fate that befell other North American tribes, in that they lost most of their original homelands. Why neighboring settlers couldn't coexist with the peaceful and adaptable Cherokee is a puzzlement.

One Eagle had ancestors and more recent family members buried in the hills surrounding Rattlesnake Springs; some of his relatives are stewards of the area. "When I go up there on the hill," he said, "I'm with my people again. I'll be talking with no one around, but it's not with myself. I know they're listening." Everyone respected One Eagle's privacy as he took a solo walk through the pasture and up to the rocky hilltop. It was one of his pilgrimages.

The next morning, I walked the journey's last miles alone. With the fourth long walk of my life ending, a sense of completion overwhelmed me. Images of countless people and places flooded my mind. I remembered those guiding visions, Bear Heart's help, the sun dance, Cheyenne's birth, and other recent events.

No large group of people awaited my journey's end in Rattlesnake Springs—no reporters, no photographers, no awards ceremony. Only One Eagle stood there, his big hand outstretched. "Thank you for walking for my Indian people," he said sincerely. My heart swelled with pride. Closing my eyes, I saw many smiling faces.

It was not until several years later, while I was chaperoning a group of young people in North Carolina, that the spiritual significance of the Trails of Tears Walk hit home. We were camping where an old Cherokee village had once stood near the present-day Qualla Boundary, along the Nantahala River. It was late. The young people were asleep or pretending to be asleep. I had smoked my medicine pipe as Bear Heart had taught me to do and lay watching the moon and her brothers and sisters, the star nations, glow in the endless depths of the sky kingdom. They seemed brighter than I remembered.

Many southeastern Indians view the Milky Way as a sacred stream upon which ancient Beings of Light once canoed to earth from the World Above. They believe the Beings gave the people many sacred teachings. On this night, anything seemed possible.

Gradually, a semi-transparent blue stream of light emerged from the sky and moved across the ground. It stretched for miles, it seemed, all the way to Oklahoma. People filled this blue corridor. They looked like old-time

Indian people. Many wore ruffled calico and gingham, woven sashes, and turbans decorated with egret plumes. Intricate beadwork and arm and breast ornaments added to their colorful attire. They were walking, but they weren't traveling west on the Trail of Tears; they were traveling east! They were walking the Trail of Tears in reverse.

From their campfires in the sky, the ancestors were returning to help heal old wounds and to awaken people from their slumber. They were coming home.

Part

FOUR

HOMELAND

Chapter
17

MOUNTAINS IN ILLINOIS

This is nuts," I said, awakening from a dream. Its images were still strong: In it, I was traveling through Illinois, the state of my birth and childhood, where in actuality I hadn't lived for thirty-five years. It was beautiful country; the sap of summer was flowing strongly. And oddly, I saw mountains, high mountains in land once known for its vast prairies.

Later, I couldn't shake the dream. It had come during a major transition in my life, in that I was about to lose my job. Funding for the government magazine where I worked, *Florida Wildlife*, had been cut by the state legislature after fifty-six years of publication. Change was occurring—and now a vision of mountains in Illinois!

When I opened an Illinois map, several places jumped out at me, and memories filled me with emotion. One place of my youth was prominent—a remnant prairie across the street from my former home in Arlington Heights, near

Chicago. We had called the span of waist-high grasses and wildflowers "the field." There had been no signs barring entry to the field, no fences; we never knew who owned it. In many ways, it was our land, belonging to the children of the area. We knew it best.

There, my friends and I could play games of hide and seek, glimpse rabbits and meadowlarks, pick strawberries, and marvel at the fireflies doing what Edwin Way Teale called "the dance of . . . winged lanterns."[1] The field was a place of wonder, a place for solace, where a young boy who sought wild things could feel free.

A wildfire once swept across the field, rumored to have been started by kids playing with matches. It nearly burned the entire expanse before firemen raced out and beat the flames into submission with what looked to be rubber mats on sticks. We weren't sure if the blackened land marked the end of our beloved grassland—the smell of burnt grass lingered for days—but the prairie turned green again, more lush than before. It was my first chance to see fire as a force of renewal.

We built a fort in an oak tree that rose above the remnant prairie. Perched in the upper limbs, we could look out over the prairie and sway with the wind, feel sap rising through bark and observe how the tree's pulse slackened in fall and quickened in spring. We saw how the tree bled when we impaled living wood with nails. We often pondered how we could build a fort without wounding the tree, sometimes experimenting with ropes, but an accident changed everything. A boy slipped from a high limb and busted his head. The neighborhood men formed a type of eco-lynch mob and cut down the oak, its massive limbs stripped to a bare trunk of amputated stubs.

Exposed on the prairie for decades, having withstood countless fires and storms, our tree was no match against the chainsaw and the attitude it represented. We mourned the loss.

Over the years, the field became smaller as rows of houses were built in the eastern section. Other fields in the area disappeared entirely. Soon, little open space separated our town from others.

In 1968, when I was eleven, my father took a job in Florida. Before we left, I said goodbye to what remained of the field. It had become an almost daily companion—a friend to be missed.

As the years passed and my family acclimated to our new existence, little drew us back to our former home. My Illinois grandparents passed away. Other relatives moved to Florida. I gradually lost touch with boyhood friends. The ties had been broken, or so I thought. And then, thirty-five years later, I had that dream, the dream of mountains in Illinois. It was time to go back.

I embarked for "The Prairie State" in 2003 with my daughter Cheyenne, now seventeen, and her friend, Torrey. So that we could pile gear in the passenger side of the front seat of my sedan, they occupied the back seat. I felt like a chauffeur.

The girls mostly read, slept, and played cards as we crossed the backbone of the Appalachian Mountains in Tennessee, trying to outrun tropical storm Bill. Bill was a pesky fellow; we only eluded the driving rains when we reached Illinois. Very few tropical storms encroach upon midwestern cornfields. The sky bore only puffy white clouds; there were no mountainous masses, as in my dream. Still, it was apparent that farm fields had received ample rain in recent weeks. Corn stalks were deep green, even lush looking. Wildflowers and tall grasses rimmed the fields. It was a rich Illinois summer.

Turning west onto Highway 50, I hoped to make it to my father's hometown of Pana by nightfall. Pana is a small central Illinois town where my grandfather served as town doctor and mayor and where my father played halfback on the high school football team. From Arlington Heights, we used to visit every summer. I knew every street.

My earliest memory, in fact, was of something that happened in Pana. When barely three years old, I had been walking through my grandparents' house. My grandfather, Pop, was lying on the couch. He wasn't feeling well, and I was careful to be quiet. What I didn't understand was that Pop was dying.

As I walked past him, in silence, our eyes met. Pop smiled weakly. He captured me in his gaze, and—at three—I felt the love.

Some say one's first memory can be auspicious. Mine took place in that brief moment when young and old regarded each other for the last time, each moving on to a different existence. That was my only memory of my grandfather, but I've seen the symbolism of our meeting play out again and again in the meeting of old and new, with both sides benefiting from mutual love and respect.

Now, as we drove down Highway 50, the road triggered other memories, too. In 1984, our cross-continental Walk for the Earth had covered the width of Illinois on this highway, once an east-west path for migrating bison. I had thought then of taking a side trip to Pana, but I hadn't wanted to leave the other walkers. After five months of traveling together, we had coalesced into a close-knit community of about twenty-five people.

On that walk, we had experienced the magic of becoming a cohesive group that moved in harmony with the earth and each other. It felt good. We shared meals, picked each other up when we were down or tired, and politely closed our ears to more intimate sounds after dark. To reach that point, we had endured months of personality clashes, a seemingly inevitable occurrence when people are thrust together in sometimes stressful situations for long periods. But we had persevered and prospered.

When we had walked through Illinois, we had camped in town parks, churchyards, and fallow fields. We had traversed a rolling patchwork of farms and trees, interspersed with small towns such as Lebanon, Carlyle, Odin, and Salem. Although there were no prairies, we had enjoyed picturesque silos, barns, and mostly white farmhouses with big, inviting front porches. People were friendly. The first hints of fall had touched the land. Even on foot, we felt that our trek through Illinois had raced by too quickly. Part of my journal during that period read:

9/9/84: We camp at a Lion's Club park in Summerfield, and we are grateful for their pavilion and meeting hall. It begins to storm. A military man with a crew cut is the Lion's Club president. He disagrees with many of our views but maintains that the Lion's Club bylaws state that we must promote open dialogue among people. Evidently, several Lion's Club members, fearing vandalism, expressed opposition to our staying here. But the man has boldly vouched for us. With coffee mug in hand, he allays their fears by staying the entire rain-filled night. 'I'm working on them,' he says, 'They'll come around.' But, as are many others, he is surprised that we walked through East St. Louis and lived to tell about it. Our main image of East St. Louis, though, is of several people approaching to shake our hands.

Two days after I had made this entry, I summarized the experience this way:

A seven-month walk means wrinkled, wet feet; hot, swelling, blistered feet; feet that feel like ice blocks; feet that are always smelly. It includes the ecstasy of a foot massage, the warmth of a hug or of twelve or twenty hugs, the satisfied bone-tired feeling at day's end, and the exhilaration of morning. We've had a chance to pass gossip in a small-town café and ponder the insanity of our bustling cities from a still space. We've had time truly to experience the cycle of seasons, to explode with freedom, to be a playful child, to dream, to overcome fear and limitation, and to feel that we might be able to help heal this planet by opening up to others and cleaning up our own emotional garbage. I have found solitude in open country; vulnerability when roaring, buffeting semis pass; and comfort in a group circle. These seven months that seem like seven years will one day be a cherished memory, and I'll wonder where the time went by...

That the impetus for the walk had come from a vision wouldn't be unusual in some cultures; it is in Western society. Now, traveling through Illinois again nineteen years later, I was following yet another vision—this one having come in the form of my powerful dream. I was looking for mountains where prairies once existed, knowing from experience that such visionary images should not be ignored.

At Sandoval, fulfilling what I had wanted to do in 1984, I turned north onto Highway 51 and headed for Pana. On the way, I envisioned the warm way my Aunt Mary had welcomed us to her home. After my grandparents had died, she and her family were our last relatives to remain for a while in Pana. My brother Dave and I were close in age to her three sons. These country cousins of ours played openly with fireworks, rode mini-bikes, and shot BB guns. They were a little wild, and Dave and I loved it.

But aside from wanting to revisit the sites of childhood memories, my motive for returning to Pana was to see a relatively new addition (other than the intrusive Wal-Mart). It was Anderson Prairie Park, so designated in 1986 by the city primarily due to the efforts of high school science teacher Dave Nance. The mile-long park stretches along the old Illinois Central rail bed leading to Taylorville and is one of the best examples of mesic tallgrass prairie in this part of Illinois. Because people generally left them alone, rail beds and cemeteries are some of the last places where native prairie species can be found. Dave Nance sent me his account about how the park came about:

> I was sitting in the teachers' lounge one fall day in 1984 when there was a knock at the door and someone said, "Mr. Nance, a man is here who wants to know something about the Illinois Central railroad and the plants

out there." Hence I met Gary Colin, who asked if anyone had ever thought about taking care of and developing the prairie that still existed along the railroad running south out of Pana. He said that some pretty good prairie remnants still survived there and that it could be an educational place for students.

My mind flashed back to a time when I was twelve years old. I had started a butterfly collection with the help of my brother, and we spent many hot summer days running through that same Illinois Central prairie. I began to visualize what a great project it would be to develop an outdoor laboratory where students could see nature up close and have the same experiences I had had as a boy. I knew nothing about prairies, I admitted to Gary, even though I was a science teacher who had lived all my life in the prairie state. Gary understood and agreed to accompany me to the area to begin pointing out the different plants he had found there. That trip kindled an interest that has never waned.

With volunteer help, Nance and successive classes of science students began the slow process of restoring the prairie and establishing a guided walking trail. They began to burn the prairie, mimicking natural fires, and aggressively to remove exotic vegetation and encroaching trees and brush.

"Prairies today are under immense pressure from surrounding disturbed areas to convert to woodlands and to be overtaken by nonnative weeds," said Nance. "Prairie plants are perennials for the most part and come up each year from roots that may be hundreds of years old. They tend to grow more slowly than many of the invading plants from other areas and can be overwhelmed by fast-growing annuals such as giant ragweed and sweet clover or fast-growing perennials like bush honeysuckle."

The prairie responded favorably to the management efforts. Several rare and endangered plants were found: slender ladies' tresses, green-fringed orchid, wood lily, and ear-leaved false foxglove. Rare prairie cicadas became common, and an even rarer pygmy cicada was discovered. "Abraham Lincoln traveled through Pana on the Illinois Central," said Nance, "and his view of the prairie from a railroad coach car was the same as ours today."

During our visit on a July morning, Anderson Prairie Park was a panorama of color. Blooming butterfly milkweed, coneflower, and yellow fields of false sunflowers gave me a glimpse of what it must have been like to wander for miles through tallgrass prairie, each growing season showing off its own blooms.

A small guidebook helped us identify several species that had surely grown in my boyhood prairie in Arlington Heights—little and big bluestems, asters, spiked lobelia, violets, black-eyed Susans, bluets, slender mountain mint, goldenrod, rattlesnake master, Ohio spiderwort, smooth sumac, wild strawberry, Jerusalem artichoke, New Jersey tea, Downy gentian, pale beardtongue, cream false indigo, and Indian grass. Some species I recognized from my boyhood, or from familiar Florida environments. I wasn't sure about others. All had the familiarity about them of old friends. I even began sneezing, just as I had done as a child.

If former Pana mayor John Hagler Alderson were alive to see this blooming prairie meadow, revived by teachers and students and now a recognized state natural reserve, he would have been proud. Had it come about through a sense of ecological guilt? Perhaps. Nevertheless, a small town, established in 1856 in the heart of the Illinois prairie, had developed enough awareness to embrace and revive part of its natural heritage.

Walking the streets of Pana, I saw it in a different light than I had as a boy, especially after my walk through the prairie. Now it seemed more like a prairie town than a farm town. I searched for familiar landmarks and found them. Eventually, we walked past the single-story, yellow-brick city hall. "My grandfather was mayor of Pana in the early 1940s," I told Cheyenne and Torrey. "Maybe this building was here then. Let's go inside." The girls were quiet but agreeable. They were going along with my desire to see boyhood memoryscapes with the caveat that I would then take them to Chicago. Living in a rural area, they were fascinated with big cities.

Inside the city hall, on a brown-paneled wall, a bronze plaque greeted visitors: "City Hall building dedicated 1941." Below was a list of names, the top one reading, "John H. Alderson, Mayor." I shivered and rubbed my hands over it.

"See, Cheyenne. Proof!"

"That's really neat," she exclaimed, sounding sincere. Any time you can impress a teenager, it's a victory.

When we left Pana, I felt a sense of satisfaction. Some of my people had left a mark; and, like memories of bygone days, prairie plants were now blooming again where few had bloomed for many years.

Chapter
18

CORN

After leaving Pana, we headed west on Illinois farm roads. Everywhere, corn and soybean fields stretched to the horizon and beyond.

Illinois is number one or two in corn production, and the reason is simple: prairie soils. For eight to ten thousand years after the glaciers retreated, the prairies built up a dark soil, thick and rich in organic matter. Prairie grasses range in height from two to twelve feet and have extensive root systems. When the tops of grasses and some roots die each year, or frequent fires burn them, they return nutrients to the soil. The decaying grasses contain less acid than the decaying leaves and wood of a forest environment. A higher mineral content is the result, because there is less acid to mix with rainwater and leach out the minerals. It all translates into one thing—abundance.

When I was growing up, by midsummer we could buy ripe sweet corn from roadside stands for a dime an ear, or less. At a family feast, eating four or five ears in a sitting was common. Summer was a time for corn gluttony. And we children not only ate corn, we also played with it. Across from my house was a farmer's field that grew hard yellow field corn for feeding animals. We'd pick the ripe ears and have corn battles, or, being more creative, we'd make designs with cobs on the ground.

After moving to Florida, I regarded corn in a different way as I came to know traditional Muskogee Creek Indians and their summer Green Corn Ceremony. In contrast to our own calendar, the calendar of the Muskogee Creeks revolves around corn. The Green Corn Ceremony, usually held in June in the Deep South, marks the Muskogee new year, when the first crop of corn is realized. This ceremony highlights corn as the main food staple grown by the southeastern people for more than a thousand years. Preceding the ceremony is a season-long fast from all obvious corn products. An exception is made for corn syrup, a sweetener in everything from soda to cereal. The corn fast is a way to honor and recognize corn's importance.

Because the Green Corn Ceremony celebrates the turn of the year and symbolizes a new beginning, it is a time when all crimes short of murder are forgiven and old household belongings are burned, so that people may start the year renewed and refreshed. In this way, the ceremony's emergence helped to end decades of festering intertribal feuds and clan warfare.

Charles Hudson in *The Southeastern Indians* accurately summed up the ceremony's importance: "We would have something approaching the Green Corn Ceremony if we combined Thanksgiving, New Year's festivities, Yom

Kippur, Lent, and Mardi Gras."[1] Fortunately, we do not have to speak of the ceremony in the past tense. It is still observed in various forms by most surviving tribes of the Southeast.

On the last night of the Green Corn Ceremony at the grounds I attend, participants keep an all-night vigil around the sacred fire, one that begins with dancing and story-telling. Eventually, those who become tired leave the circle. For those who remain, it is time for quiet contemplation. At ceremonial grounds where there are more participants, people often stomp dance until dawn.

During the vigil, the coming year is considered to be moving through the birth canal, with its emergence marked by the sunrise. At the moment of dawn, a silent stomp dance is performed, with sharp, spiraling turns to sym-bolize the cutting of an umbilical cord. The New Year has been born!

I've participated in several Green Corn vigils. As I have sat quietly by the fire in the wee hours, the flames have seemed to reveal what is needed—a direction, a memory, images of people and places. Images of Illinois prairies have come to me on more than one occasion, reflecting how it was long ago—vast and wild. Perhaps age-old images are difficult for the land completely to erase. At the Muskogee ceremonials, the sacred fire is considered more than a fire. It is a conduit for the One Above, the Creator, and anything is possible.

Those who have not participated in the vigil generally show their appreciation to those who have by giving them coins or a dollar bill. Once, having retired to my tent soon after the sun's first rays had touched the new fire, I repeatedly heard footsteps near my tent and the sound of falling coins. Someone had placed a paper plate by my tent door with "Thanks" written on it. When I peeked out, the plate was full of money. Happy New Year!

Most come to the Creek Indian ceremonials with a spiritual thirst, quenched by fasting, dancing, herbal medicines, and spiritual kinship. The Creek ways are age-old methods of spiritual connectedness, honed to specificity by available plants, weather patterns, and geography. Each ceremonial site is different, yet all of them are the same in their purpose—to purify and make well. Additionally, it is to become part of creation.

The Illinois Native Americans—tribes of the Illini confederation along with the Miami, Sauk, Fox, Kickapoo, Potawatomi, and those before them—had similar ways of honoring corn. Like the bison and other animals, corn represented more than a food simply to be eaten. There was a ritualistic way to plant it, grow it, and harvest it. No food source was taken for granted.

Black Hawk of the Sauk (1767–1838) described in his autobiography how the people of his village honored the corn they planted along the Rock River in northeastern Illinois. "Our women plant the corn, and as soon as they are done we make a feast, at which we dance the crane dance in which they join us, dressed in their most gaudy attire and decorated with feathers. At this feast the young men select the women they wish to have for wives." Black Hawk went on to say that, when the corn was nearly ripe:

> Our young people watch with anxiety for the signal to
> pull roasting ears, as none dare touch them until the

proper time. When the corn is fit for use another great ceremony takes place, with feasting and returning thanks to the Great Spirit for giving us corn. . . . We next have our great ball play, from three to five hundred on a side play this game [a type of lacrosse]. We play for guns, lead, horses and blankets, or any other kind of property we may have. The successful party takes the stakes, and all return to our lodges with peace and friendship. We next commence horse racing, and continue our sport and feasting until the corn is secured. We then prepare to leave our village for our hunting grounds.[2]

Buffalo Bird Woman, a Hidatsa Native American living along the Missouri River, wrote this about corn in her 1917 autobiography, *Buffalo Bird Woman's Garden*: "We cared for our corn in those days as we would care for a child. . . . We thought that our growing corn liked to hear us sing, just as children liked to hear their mother sing to them."[3]

I myself sometimes sing to my corn at home—not loudly, for fear of drawing attention, but quietly. It doesn't always keep storms from blowing over the stalks or ants from invading the cobs, but it feels good. Maybe the corn likes it, too.

Almost every Native American tribe that grew corn has their own tale of corn's origin. Not surprisingly, these tales generally involve a spiritual deity. Jackson Lewis, the grandfather of one of Bear Heart's Muskogee teachers, told a story of a woman washing and rubbing her feet, whereupon corn sprang from them. She told friends to build a corncrib and lock her in it for four days. They followed her instructions and, on the fourth day, "heard a great rumbling like distant thunder."

When they opened the crib, it was full of corn. The woman then instructed the people about how to plant and prepare it.

Some New England tribes believed that corn was first delivered by a crow or black bird, or brought to the people by a deity. Other New England tribal tales describe corn as coming from a beautiful woman with long light hair, and when silk is seen on the cornstalk, the people know the beautiful woman has not forgotten them.

Black Hawk told this story of corn's origin that comes from his people, the Sauk:

According to tradition handed down to our people, a beautiful woman was seen to descend from the clouds, and alight upon the earth, by two of our ancestors who had killed a deer and were sitting by a fire roasting a part of it to eat. They were astonished to see her, and concluded that she was hungry and had smelt the meat. They immediately went to her, taking with them a piece of the roasted venison. . . . She ate it, telling them to return to the spot where she was sitting at the end of one year, and they would find a reward for their kindness and generosity. She then ascended to the clouds and disappeared. The men returned to their village, and explained to the tribe what they had seen, done and heard, but were laughed at by their people. When the period had arrived for them to visit this consecrated ground, where they were to find a reward for their attention to the beautiful woman of the clouds, they went with a large party, and found [that] where her right hand had rested on the ground [was now] growing corn; where the left hand had rested, beans; and, immediately where she had been seated, tobacco.[4]

Other Native American tribes have different versions of the corn-woman story. Associating corn with a woman, especially its silk, seems appropriate from a biological view. The silks hanging from the husks are receptors. Each thread of silk must be fertilized by pollen in order for fruit or kernels to develop.

Corn belongs to the grass family and was first used as food at least seven thousand years ago in Mexico. Gradually, it spread across the Americas. Through natural selection and experimentation, early Native Americans helped to develop corn and its many varieties: dent, flint, flour, sweet, and waxy, as well as popcorn. Corn depends upon human—or, some would say, divine—intervention to reseed itself. Of course, modern farmers have developed hybrids and continue to experiment with variations. Corn has become a worldwide staple, and the once-vast midwestern prairies have become a renowned breadbasket.

Unlike modern farmers, though, Native Americans rarely tilled the prairies. They didn't possess the tools or the work animals to break up the tough turf. Instead, just as Black Hawk's people had done along the Rock River, the natives typically cleared gardens in the soft river bottoms using axes and hoes made from stone, bone, and wood. These gardens were convenient, too, since their villages were largely along rivers. Rivers served as travel and trade routes, and they were sources of water and food. The prairies were more for hunting bison, elk, and deer and for gathering herbs and wild plant foods.

After the Europeans had arrived, the farming of Illinois prairies began rather timidly. The French and English of the seventeenth and eighteenth centuries were mostly explorers, missionaries, soldiers, fur trappers, and traders, not farmers. The situation didn't change until the arrival of the American settlers following the Louisiana Purchase of 1803, when Illinois was claimed by the United States. These pioneers primarily came from heavily forested areas south and east of Illinois. Their accounts describe the prairies as lonely, forbidding places where one could feel engulfed by a vast sea of grass. Winters were severe, wells were difficult to dig deep enough, and there was no wood for cabins, fences, or fuel. As an added stress, Indian tribes still roamed the prairies, frequently burning areas during autumn bison hunts. Just as the Indian settlements had been, the first American settlements on the prairie were often along rivers and forest edges, where the ground was soft for planting and wood was readily available. Only gradually did prairie settlers improvise and begin using coal for fuel and hedges or ditches for fencing.

In fact, the Black Hawk War of 1832 was fought, in part, over the edge of the Rock River in Illinois where the Sauk tribe lived and planted their corn. More than twenty-five years before the outbreak of the war, the Sauks had lost their lands in a disputed treaty signed in St. Louis, one of hundreds of questionable and fraudulent treaties between the Indian nations and the European and American governments. Black Hawk refused to recognize its legitimacy. He and his people stubbornly held onto their ancestral lands, even when settlers moved in and began plowing and fencing his cornfields, claiming the land as their own.

"My reason teaches me that land cannot be sold," said Black Hawk. "The Great Spirit gave it to his children to live upon and cultivate as far as necessary for their subsistence, and so long as they occupy and cultivate it they have the right to the soil, but if they voluntarily leave it, then any other people have the right to settle on it. Nothing can be sold but such things as can be carried away."[5]

At first, white and Indian farmers tried to farm side by side, an arrangement that proved unsatisfactory to both parties. "Our people were treated very badly by the whites on many occasions," said Black Hawk. "At one time a white man beat one of our women cruelly, for pulling a few suckers of corn out of his field to suck when she was hungry. At another time one of our young men was beat with clubs by two white men, for opening a fence which crossed our road to take his horse through. His shoulder blade was broken and his body badly bruised, from the effects of which he soon after died."[6] Black Hawk also complained of white people bringing whiskey into the village and cheating drunken Indians out of their horses, guns, and traps.

Black Hawk made frequent appeals to government authorities, but when little was done, the chief made an astute observation: "How smooth must be the language of the whites, when they can make right look like wrong, and wrong like right."[7]

Tensions mounted during every planting season, with government leaders urging Black Hawk to leave his Illinois village forever and move across the Mississippi, citing the disputed treaties as proof of their authority. Finally, in 1832, when Black Hawk defied the American authorities and crossed the Mississippi from Iowa Territory in order once again to plant corn and beans along the Rock River, his presence set off widespread panic. The white settlers feared an invasion. Army regulars were put into the field, and Illinois governor John Reynolds called up the state militia, a militia that included young Abraham Lincoln. Lincoln was elected captain of his New Salem unit, his first leadership position. He never saw action, but he commented later, in an 1859 autobiography, that his three months in the field were "a success which gave me more pleasure than any I have had since."[8]

Thousands of soldiers chased Black Hawk and his band across northern Illinois and southern Wisconsin. The war lasted through the summer, only ending when Black Hawk was forced to surrender. Most of his people had been killed—and all over a two-mile stretch of cornfield.

In grade school in Arlington Heights, we learned more about Squanto than about Black Hawk, maybe because Squanto had taught settlers how to plant corn and survive in the "New World," while Black Hawk had inspired the settlers' worst fears.

In 1832, the same year the Black Hawk War was fought, my great-great-grandfather John Carroll Hagler left Tennessee with his uncle West Peak to settle in Illinois. John was thirteen at the time. I have often wondered if they were involved in the conflict. Did they, as did so many others, view the outcome as simply part of America's Manifest Destiny? And were bison, elk, wolves, and other abundant wildlife still roaming an American Serengeti, or were they, too, being driven off or killed?

With the Indians gone, it was the beginning of the end of the Illinois prairie. Progress was viewed as anything that transformed the grassy wilderness into a "fruited plain."

The challenge united people, and a young John Deere revolutionized the cause. Lured by tales of golden opportunity in "the West," Deere left Vermont in the mid-1830s and set up a blacksmith business in Grand Detour, Illinois. He quickly ascertained that the rich midwestern topsoil frustrated farmers because they had to scrape soil from their cast-iron plows every few feet. Many were ready to give up and return to the more sandy eastern or southern soils.

Using steel from a broken saw blade, Deere fashioned the first self-scouring steel plow, along with a properly shaped moldboard. Ten years later, Deere was producing a thousand steel plows a year. The conversion of the prairie into cornfields had begun in earnest.

The early homesteaders couldn't have known that the massive transformation of the midwestern prairie—thirty-seven million acres in Illinois alone—would result in huge releases of carbon into the atmosphere, contributing to global warming. Even today, few people make the correlation, not realizing that the soils went from containing ten percent carbon to less than three percent after being plowed. And how could the early homesteaders have known that the rich soils could be depleted? After extensive farming, they would remain dark in color, but denser, with less organic matter. Fertilization, once unheard of, became a necessity.

By the late twentieth century, more than ninety-nine percent of the prairie would be plowed or paved over, leaving an estimated one-hundredth of one percent. Ironically, it was the Indians' corn that would still dominate the once-vast hunting lands of the Sauk, Fox, Kickapoo, Potawatomi, Miami, and Illini nations.

Chapter 19

PRAIRIE!

In contrast to the beleaguered pioneers who found the prairie harsh and forbidding, early poets, writers, and botanists had a different reaction. In 1833, William Cullen Bryant's first exposure to the grasslands was intense and emotional. He begins his poem "The Prairies" this way:

These are the gardens of the Desert, these
The unshorn fields, boundless and beautiful,
For which the speech of England has no name—
The Prairies. I behold them for the first,
And my heart swells, while the dilated sight
Takes in the encircling vastness. Lo! they stretch
In airy undulations, far away,
As if the Ocean, in his gentlest swell,
Stood still, with all his rounded elbows fixed,
And motionless forever...[1]

Eliza Steele, one of many early pioneers who left the eastern seaboard for the midwestern prairies, waxed eloquently about the prairie in the journal she kept during her 1840 wagon journey across Illinois:

> Imagine yourself in the center of an immense circle of velvet herbage, the sky for its boundary upon every side; the whole clothed with a radiant efflorescence of every brilliant hue. We rode thus through a perfect wilderness of sweets, sending forth perfume, and animated with myriads of glittering birds and butterflies. . . . We passed whole acres of blossoms all bearing one hue, as purple, perhaps, or masses of yellow or rose; and then again a carpet of every color intermixed, or narrow bands, as if a rainbow had fallen upon the verdant slopes. . . . It was, in fact, a vast garden.[2]

Botanist C. W. Short was equally moved by the Illinois prairie, as evidenced in a letter to a colleague in 1845: "Thus from some elevated position in a large prairie the eye is literally empurpled with the flowering spikes of several species of *Liatrus* [blazing star]."[3]

The difference wrought by a mere 150 years of urbanization is highlighted by these 1949 observations by Aldo Leopold: "I am sitting in a 60-mile-an-hour bus sailing over a highway originally laid out for horse and buggy. The ribbon of concrete has been widened and widened until the field fences threaten to topple into the road cuts. In the narrow thread of sod between the shaved banks and the toppling fences grow the relics of what once was Illinois: the prairie."[4]

Now, on my 2003 journey with Cheyenne and Torrey, as we approached the Illinois capital city of Springfield, the farm roads widened, and few if any prairie flowers or grasses could be seen between the fences and the asphalt. Like many midwestern towns and cities, an old part of Springfield revealed gritty railroad yards and redbrick buildings covered in faded advertisements. Each generation had left a mark.

We passed through the small city with little problem and soon stopped at New Salem, where Abraham Lincoln had spent several years as a young man. New Salem, situated along the Sangamon River, harbors an 1830s-era log cabin village reconstructed primarily by the Civilian Conservation Corps in the 1930s. William Cullen Bryant wrote about the Sangamon country during his excursion across central Illinois. His "The Painted Cup" begins:

> The fresh savannas of the Sangamon.
> Here rise in gentle swells, and the long grass
> Is mixed with rustling hazels. Scarlet tufts
> Are glowing in the green, like flakes of fire;
> The wanderers of the prairie know them well.
> And call the brilliant flower the Painted Cup.[5]

Wandering around New Salem's log structures and past numerous gardens and farm animals was a journey into the past, in more ways than one. I had visited New Salem as a boy, more than thirty-five years before, and it had changed little. It seemed I was finding pleasure in things that appeared unchanged in a world where change can be fast and sometimes cruel.

In the midst of New Salem, a doe ran across our path, reminding us of the wild. She leaped over a tall wooden fence, temporarily leaving her spotted fawn behind.

We made our way to Goose Lake Prairie State Natural Area just south of the Illinois River, near Interstate 57. At 2,537 acres, it is currently the largest tallgrass prairie east of the Mississippi. Although two power plants loom in the distance, here one can grasp the expansiveness of former prairie lands. From certain angles, only prairie can be seen.

Beside a small glacial pond, where sandpipers fed, stood the reconstructed log cabin of the Cragg family. There was a peaceful feeling about the place, enhanced by an incessant wind that seemed part of the land. The wind would frequently shift direction and intensity, rustling grass with subtle differences in tone.

Viewing the prairie-framed cabin elicited a type of frontier memory. On a basic level, I sensed the joys, sorrows, and struggles of the early homesteaders. The frontier cabin served as a birthing room, hospital, convalescent home, and mortuary, often simultaneously.

The Cragg cabin originally stood ten miles from Goose Lake Prairie, along the Mazon River. The Craggs had built it in the 1830s, and, because they added a second-story loft, it was called "the palace." Situated halfway between Chicago and Bloomington, it became a favorite stopover for travelers and cowboys driving cattle.

The Craggs' pioneer children often played with grandchildren of the Potawatomi chief Shabbona. Shabbona's band summered along the Mazon River. It is a pleasant scene to visualize, red and white children enjoying wild country together—fishing, boating, climbing trees, and venturing into the prairie to wander, pick strawberries, and hunt. But the harsh realities of the Indian Removal period of the 1830s and 40s made for a tragic backdrop.

Chief Shabbona, a broad man whose name is believed to mean "strong built like a bear," gained a fierce reputation when he fought alongside Tecumseh in an effort to drive Americans from Indian lands. At age nineteen, he became the youngest chief of any Potawatomi village. But Tecumseh's death at the Battle of the Thames in Ontario prompted Shabbona to rethink his strategy regarding the young American nation. When Black Hawk sought Shabbona's alliance in 1832, while sharing a traditional dog feast, Shabbona was unsympathetic.

"Join me," Black Hawk reportedly said, "and our warriors will be as numerous as the trees in the forest."

Shabbona coldly replied, "And the army of the pale faces you will have to encounter will be as numerous as the leaves of those trees."

His words proved prophetic.

Perhaps fearing a backlash against all Illinois Indians, Shabbona had warned settlers of the imminent fighting that was to occur with Black Hawk's presence east of the Mississippi. Nevertheless, four years later, the "Trail of Death" for the Potawatomi began; many were forcibly marched to lands west of the Mississippi. Shabbona stayed, having been allotted 1,280 acres in DeKalb County in the 1829 Treaty of Prairie du Chien, land that included the wooded "prairie island" where his people's village once stood. But when Shabbona visited the relocated Potawatomi in Kansas sometime after 1848, his land was declared abandoned and sold to speculators. Upon his return, white friends gave him twenty acres on the Illinois River, where he lived on a small pension until his death in 1859.

He was one of the last Potawatomi to live in Illinois. If he were here today, or if his spirit could speak, I wonder what he would say.

Part of Shabbona's original land allotment has become the DeKalb County Forest Preserve; and, like ghosts from the past, in 1998 some of Shabbona's descendants from the Prairie Band Potawatomi of Kansas returned to reclaim the land. Two treaties had been violated when it was sold to speculators, they maintained.

Nervous Illinois officials, fearing a casino, refuted the claim. "The contention of the state is that they [the Potawatomi] don't have a legitimate claim to make, that there are no indigenous Native American tribes existing in Illinois, nor have there been for over one hundred years," said Thomas Hardy, spokesperson for the governor.[6]

The Illinois Indian wars may have begun all over again.

Still awaiting a federal Interior Department ruling on their land claim, the Prairie Band Potawatomi took matters in their own hands in April 2006 when they purchased 128 acres of the contested 1,280 acres of ancestral land for almost $9 million. Local residents and public officials assumed a casino was in the works, since the tribe runs a casino on their Kansas reservation. "You wouldn't spend [more than] $8 million to raise corn on it," said Dennis Sands, vice chairman of the DeKalb County Board.[7] If the tribe does pursue building a casino, a goal they have not confirmed publicly since acquiring the property, it would require a lengthy series of regulatory steps with state and federal officials that could take years.

Chief Shabbona likely hunted the Goose Lake Prairie. After his death, the prairie was spared from farming, mainly because it was considered too wet in places. The remains of nineteenth-century potter's clay mining and the town of Jugtown have largely disappeared.

While Cheyenne and Torrey retreated to the coolness of the visitor's center, it being a surprisingly hot ninety-five degrees, I slurped from my water bottle and wandered among waist-high grasses. In early fall, some of these same plants would have towered over my head, and my expansive mood might have changed to near claustrophobia, especially had I been younger and shorter. Pioneer children were sometimes lost in tall prairie grass and never found. Only winter and heavy snow helped to clear the prairie, until the spring, when the cycle would begin anew.

Fire played an important role, too. Thunderstorms produced lightning that ignited wildfires, or Native Americans ignited fires during autumn bison hunts. In 1680, Father Louis Hennepin was one of the first to document the Native Americans' use of fire in this way:

> When they see a herd the Indians assemble in great numbers. They set fire to the grass all around these animals except for one passage left on purpose. There the Indians station themselves with their bows and arrows. The buffaloes, wanting to avoid the fire, are thus forced to pass by the Indians, who at times kill as many as a hundred and twenty of them in one day. The buffaloes are distributed according to the needs of the families.[8]

Sometimes, Native Americans burned prairie grass close to their villages in order to attract game. Grazing animals prefer the succulent new growth after a recent fire.

Prairie pioneers often dreaded the sweeping fires that could wipe out a homestead. They also had to contend with cook fires that could ignite their stick-and-mud chimneys and spread throughout the cabin.

Today, land managers attempt to simulate natural fires by igniting ones in late March and early April—before wildlife begins nesting and native vegetation begins to sprout. About a third of the prairie is burned each year. In the absence of fire, trees such as hawthorns and, to a lesser extent, prairie crab apple, wild plum, and quaking aspen begin to dominate the prairie's drier ridges. All were historically present in small numbers, but kept in check by fire. It isn't enough simply to protect a chunk of native prairie; it must be properly managed.

I wandered the mowed trails, hearing calls of red-winged blackbirds, robins, and possibly the endangered Henslow's sparrow. Not surprisingly, most species of animals that primarily depend upon prairie habitat are either threatened or endangered. Even insects, more than a thousand different species, rely on remnant prairies. They range from native leafhoppers, planthoppers, and treehoppers to moths, dragonflies, and butterflies.

Below the surface, too, life abounds. Long roots and soil are hosts to mycorrhizal fungi, mites, amoebas, nematodes, springtails, bacteria, pseudoscorpions, earthworms, wireworms, sawbugs, millipedes, ants, larvae, moles, and numerous other species. A recent study found twenty thousand life forms in one thimbleful of prairie soil, prompting one scientist to liken the prairie root system to an inverted rain forest in terms of biodiversity.

But you can't focus on the unseen for long when walking through a living prairie during the growing season. Blooms of the white wild indigo, pasture rose, wild quinine, and tufted hairgrass all competed for my attention. About half of the more than eight hundred species of plants documented in tallgrass prairie ecosystems are found at Goose Lake. Each growing season is a menagerie of color. I yearned to visit during other seasons, even in winter when snow covers the land like a frozen white sea, when the challenge is to feel the hidden power below.

Seeds from Goose Lake Prairie are helping to restore other Illinois tallgrass prairies, such as the Midewin National Tallgrass Prairie Preserve outside Wilmington. Once part of the Joliet Army Ammunition Plant, it is the nation's first national tallgrass prairie, the result of a thawing cold war. *Midewin* (mi-DAY-win) is an appropriate label for this preserve, situated on land where four billion pounds of explosives were manufactured, for it is a Potawatomi word meaning "healing."

While much of the nineteen-thousand-acre area remains closed to the public as the Army cleans up the site from decades of manufacturing and packaging explosives, information about the preserve is tantalizing naturalists. At least sixteen state-listed endangered and threatened species can be found there, and the area contains a rare dolomite prairie environment. Three largely undisturbed streams running through Midewin harbor increasingly rare species of fish and mussels. At present only a small percent of Midewin consists of native prairie vegetation, but trained professionals and volunteers have established native seed gardens that will serve to expand restoration areas.

The massive restoration planned for Midewin includes not only plants, but also the reestablishment of bison and elk, missing components on all remnant Illinois prairies. Bison! I once drove all the way to South Dakota to view bison blackening a prairie hillside. To envision a similar scene in the state of my birth fills me with anticipation.

Studies on the Nature Conservancy's Konza Prairie in Kansas point to bison as a complementary component of the prairie ecosystem. The two may be symbiotic. The bison's selective grazing helps to balance competition between forbs and dominant grasses, enhancing biodiversity. One researcher called them the keystone herbivore of North America's grasslands, as vital as fire in maintaining prairie health.

Buffalo, in turn, have learned to adapt to the prairie and elemental forces. In winter, their massive heads brush aside deep snow in order to graze. Capable of running thirty to forty-five miles per hour for sustained periods, they are fast enough to outrun most fires. After a spring fire, bison will quickly return to a burned area to feed on tender, sprouting grasses.

At several southeastern ceremonial grounds, participants still dance for the bison at sunset, even though eastern bison were extirpated more than a century ago. The shaggy beasts have not been forgotten; the dance even mimics their wallowing movements.

An estimated 160 million buffalo roamed North America at the time of Lewis and Clark's epic journey. A century later, less than a thousand remained. It was perhaps the largest animal slaughter in recorded history, their demise mirroring the fate of the midwestern prairies. Today, however, several hundred thousand bison roam public lands and private ranches. Their future hinges, in part, on the continued restoration of their former prairie habitat. If hump-backed bison should ever again blacken Illinois prairie, the land would surely rejoice!

The hope of Midewin, and of many smaller restoration projects, marks a return of the midwestern prairie, in what are now islands of biodiversity in a sea of corn, soybeans, and urban landscape. Perhaps they are the mountains in the dream I had that launched me on my journey through Illinois, symbolically representing power returning to the land. They remind me of Carl Sandburg's words, "I am the prairie, mother of men, waiting."

Chapter 20

"MY BLOOD, ITS BLOOD"

Attractive, I thought, and manicured. Except for bushy growth behind the tall fence surrounding a holding pond, nothing seemed out of place in Hasbrook Park in Arlington Heights—my boyhood park.

Taking off my sandals, I strode barefoot across the green grass. Dark earth was visible between the grass blades—prairie earth. My old house and prairie field—if it remained—was only a block away, and I could see the blue water tower that had once loomed over the landscape. In just a few minutes, I could answer many questions: How had the neighborhood changed? Was the small farm still across the road? More importantly, was anything left of the prairie?

Cheyenne, Torrey, and I walked along West Thomas Street. My old house was soon visible. It had been remodeled and was almost unrecognizable, but I was proud to see that the spindly maple I had planted was now more than thirty feet tall.

I remembered when my friend Peter and I had set up a makeshift teepee of sticks and blankets in my then-treeless yard. It had been spring, and a brisk wind was blowing. We had trouble keeping the teepee upright, and, for some reason, we sensed that Native American spirits were with us. It seemed our decade-old subdivision and manicured lawns could not suppress the innate power of the land or her native people. Perhaps we, being children—and before the age of computers, electronic games, and after-school programs—were more in touch with the land than adults were. We'd come home and quickly shed our school clothes so we could romp outside. If there were Native American spirits roaming about, they were no more out of place than the wind, the birds, or the prairie grass. It was simply part of childhood's magic.

Now, stopping at a familiar street corner, I took a deep breath and scanned across the road. No farm. No prairie. Only new houses and paved streets. At the water tower's base, I searched for any sign of prairie plants. Maybe some clumps of big and little bluestem, or Indian grass or switch grass had survived. But no; nothing was to be seen but neatly mowed grass. All that remained of our childhood prairie was the very earth upon which it had grown.

Having just roamed a large remnant prairie at Goose Lake, I now realized that the small prairie of my youth had been connected to something much broader, being part of a nearly continuous grassland that had once stretched all the way to the Rockies. It had borne the hooves and paws of countless bison, elk, and wolves, as well as the moccasins of Native Americans and the wagon wheels of early pioneers. While I had witnessed one fire sweeping across its expanse, thousands of fires had preceded it, each one a purifying, life-giving force. The field had been part of something ancient, immense, and resilient. For me, it had been an ambassador for wilderness, a connection to the Life Force.

My old friend Janisse Ray writes of going back to her southwest Georgia home in her book *Wild Card Quilt*. While her childhood landscape was one of "fierce occupation of trees," mine was of a waist-high wall of grass. Still, I felt about it even as Ray writes, "My blood, its blood."[1]

The bones and blood of a person come from the land of one's birth and upbringing. There is a type of internal recognition that occurs when one returns, like magnetized ions that recognize each other and are unavoidably drawn together. My father, for instance, once told me of a time he had driven his grandfather home to Michigan after the old man had received skin cancer surgery in Illinois. "He was subdued," said Dad. "But the closer we got to Michigan, the more energized he became. He would go on short hikes at rest stops and I worried about losing him."

As cars streamed by on my once-quiet street, I closed my eyes and dropped a few fragments of tobacco leaf, a traditional Native American gift of appreciation. Perhaps some spirit of the prairie was still there, under the lawn grass, asphalt, wood, and brick. Maybe a small plot could be reestablished where young people could touch what I had touched. Such things begin with prayer and a vision.

In rearing my own family, I had built a rustic house in a remnant longleaf pine forest south of Tallahassee. "A prairie with trees" was how early pioneers described the longleaf ecosystem, since longleaf pines were liberally spaced among tall golden grasses. One could drive a wagon cross-country for miles without the need of a cleared road or path.

In the open woodlands around my house, I frequently burned the understory to stimulate wiregrass and other native plants. I planted longleaf pine seedlings and watched them grow year by year. In my Florida yard, I found button snakeroot, brilliant orange butterfly milkweed, asters, and several other Illinois prairie species. It was my own piece of native prairie—in north Florida.

Now, on my visit back to Illinois, I was touched by the remnant prairies being protected south of Chicago. Other prairie plots are being restored in schoolyards, backyards, vacant lots, and abandoned gas stations and industrial areas, even in the city. The prairie is returning, piecemeal, emerging as bastions of hope and healing. Its small plots are the physical manifestations of the dreams and visions of many people.

Later, on the way to the motel, Cheyenne and Torrey and I spotted a sign along Arlington Heights Road that said "Prairie Park." Maybe a stretch of prairie still survived in Arlington Heights, I thought, having somehow escaped the mad rush to urbanize. Perhaps it was one of the small prairies being restored by the Chicago Wilderness Coalition, a network of almost two hundred landowners, businesses, government bodies, and conservation and civic groups dedicated to establishing green space in the nation's third largest metropolitan area.

"Why would they call it Prairie Park if it isn't a prairie?" I asked the girls, turning onto the side road where the sign pointed.

"I bet it's not," said Cheyenne skeptically. Torrey agreed. I wanted to prove them wrong. The first suburbs had advertised country living within easy reach of the city, but the "country" had quickly been trampled. Perhaps that trend could be reversed.

The road ended at a parking lot. When we pulled in, we saw that "Prairie Park" consisted of baseball diamonds. I shouldn't have been surprised. "Prairie" was a frequent misnomer in an area where suburbs bear descriptive names such as Rolling Meadows and Des Plaines. Today, their only resemblance to native prairies is in their names.

Perhaps a time will come when true prairie parks are as numerous as baseball diamonds. If baseball is America's great pastime, then the prairie is its natural heart. It is the lifeblood of the Midwest and of every midwesterner. We need to return to it again and again to be replenished, to feed our souls. It is as vital as air.

When I was a child, Little League was a tortuous episode in which I missed far more pitches than I hit. My at-bats were confidence boosters for opposing pitchers. It was only as an adult, playing slow-pitch softball for a coed team, that I gained a sense of confidence. I enjoyed myself, and even pitched a few games. Fun became more important than competition.

When I was growing up, the prairie had always been the antithesis of competition. Whenever I went walking through the grasslands, it didn't matter if I swung a bat like Mickey Mantle or raced around the bases like Jackie Robinson. I could simply be who I was. There was a gentleness about the place, a nurturing quality. I went to the prairie never intending to gain anything from it, but I always did.

Chapter

21

GOOD MEDICINE

As planned, Cheyenne, Torrey, and I visited downtown Chicago, ending the day by seeing the acting troupe known as the Blue Man Group. The three blue mimes were bizarre but entertaining, liberally mixing their performance with strobes, black lights, drumming, and about fifty rolls of toilet paper. They were modern-day heyokas, the white world's version of sacred clowns—important in any culture as a complement to focused spiritual practice. And laughter is, after all, good medicine.

On the train ride back to the suburbs, the day's excitement subsided and a feeling of not having had closure with my old neighborhood began nagging me. I had to go back again, alone.

Just before sunrise, while the girls slept, I left the motel. Instead of taking busy Arlington Heights Road, I drove back streets, passing several churches not yet open for Sunday services. Two of them I had attended as a boy.

When my brother and I were young, Mom encouraged church attendance. She volunteered to teach our Sunday school class, hoping to infuse us that way with more enthusiasm. Our countenance on Sunday mornings, however, more resembled that in those rare moments when we were forced to clean our rooms, or change my baby brother's diaper. A boy's life is generally more suited to heathen activity, like wrestling in the living room, or romping through the field.

The field was a spiritual place, certainly, as I experienced it on a basic, subconscious level. I never equated it with religion, though; it just felt good to be there.

One Sunday morning, Dave blurted out, "We don't want to go to church." We were already dressed in our uncomfortably stiff white shirts and bow ties with matching vests.

"It's boring," I added.

Mom insisted, trying to herd us out the door. We hung back, employing a form of civil disobedience children instinctively learn. To our surprise, Dad took our side and suggested a compromise, offering us each twelve cents for every time we attended church. Twelve cents! That sum purchased either a comic book, a package of Twinkies, round snowball cakes with coconut-covered frosting, or an orange push-up ice-cream treat. Bribes for Jesus—it worked.

After a year or so of this arrangement, Dave had collected twice as many comic books as I had. My reasoning was sound. On any given Sunday, I could eat my treat and read Dave's comic soon after he finished. That's how you can have your cake and comic, too.

At age nine, I began accompanying my friend, Chuck, to his church just down the road. Our first Sunday school teacher was an ex-English soldier in World War II. He told exciting stories of desert warfare and of how the power of prayer had gotten him through several precarious situations, such as when he was trapped in a foxhole for two days. Life and death struggle—that made an impact on me. Sunday school suddenly became interesting, even powerful.

The following year we had a different teacher, a woman. She was pleasant, but the war stories ended. One Sunday, our teacher didn't show. We, the students, waited and became restless. Playfully, I hit Chuck on the head with my Bible, just as the substitute teacher walked in. The huge woman became livid. She grabbed hold of my arm and pulled me to her face. She had whiskers and bad breath. "Don't you ever do that again!" she snarled. I was petrified.

"After class, I'm gonna whip you," she vowed.

My parents never whipped me. Having psychology backgrounds, they believed in positive reinforcement, or, as punishment, in sending me to my room to ponder my behavior, followed by a serious, one-on-one discussion. Sometimes, I had yearned for a quick spanking just to get it over with.

Sitting in Sunday school that day, I now wished to be sent to my room. "Run for it," a friend behind me whispered when the teacher turned her back. As the chalk from her heavy lettering squeaked on the blackboard, I thought of bolting for the door, but I was hesitant. I could be tracked down with hounds or something. If caught, a fate bordering on crucifixion could await.

The teacher swung around and glared at me, as if reading my thoughts. It was scary. I was in a foxhole, pinned down by enemy fire. And the enemy, the size of a tank and just as intimidating, would soon advance. For the first time in my life, I began to pray, earnestly. I prayed for deliverance. I prayed for a miracle. I prayed to be anywhere else. Chuck fidgeted beside me. This was his church. He didn't want to see me get hurt. Would he witness my thrashing, or wait outside?

Just before class was over, our real teacher strode in like a divine ambassador from the Creator or the good fairy in the *Wizard of Oz* who emerged from a sparkling bubble to protect Dorothy from the wicked witch. With a grave voice, the substitute promptly told her of my blasphemy regarding God's holy book. Our teacher nodded, showing concern, but I knew she would overlook the episode. She had a compassionate heart.

In leaving, the substitute turned to me and sputtered, "You're lucky this time."

I had met the devil and dodged her violent wrath. Every time I returned to that church, I warily looked for her, but I never saw her again—except in my nightmares.

Perhaps, upon reflection, my most profound spiritual experience had not occurred in a church at all, at least not one with walls and a ceiling. It had occurred, instead, after Bear Heart had invited me to the Southern Cheyenne Sun Dance on a small stretch of grassland along Oklahoma's Canadian River. During the last night of the four-day ritual, well after midnight, the overhead stars shone like campfires on a distant prairie—millions in a clear field of black. Aromas of damp grass, wood smoke, and smoldering sage permeated the air.

As painted Cheyenne dancers bobbed up and down around a huge, forked cottonwood, my gaze joined others in becoming transfixed on the tree. The pole had become an *axis mundi*, penetrating through layers of the cosmos, from deep within the earth to the heavens. The rhythm from a circle of drummers felt like a heartbeat, and their high-pitched singing, like an eagle's cry. The shrill sound of bone whistles blown by the dancers pierced the air.

Pulsing, pulsing, the energy had continued to build until I felt in it an immense power. It was as if the unspoiled places and native people through the ages had fused as one. All was alive! Tears streamed down my face. Power came forth through the pole, rising through my feet, welling inside my chest, and beaming out through my head. It was as if I had stuck a finger into one of the earth's electrical sockets and become part of the current.

I have respectfully set foot in Christian churches since that experience, but mostly for weddings and funerals. My preference is to worship outdoors where there is beauty and wildness, especially if it is with native people or those of like mind. I appreciate having the choice.

After a leisurely drive down quiet streets in Arlington Heights, I made it to Hasbrook Park for the sunrise. As I propped myself against a tree, facing east, a cool breeze sent chill bumps up my arm. I felt the prairie earth; it was damp from the previous night's rain. The grass was greener. Breathing was easy.

Most noticeable were the birds—mockingbirds and others. They seemed happy. They were greeting the dawn as they have always done, singing from every tree. Some species can adapt.

Bear Heart once told a story about having sat and held a tree for hours as part of his medicine training. At first, he felt self-conscious—what would people think? Then, after a while, almost imperceptibly at first, that tree began to talk to him, and he became absorbed in the communication.

Mother Earth speaks to those who listen, and listening can only occur by being still. The Creeks and the Seminoles believe that when one reaches a certain point in medicine training, the healing plants sing to you. This first happened to me in the back of my property. On a slow walk, sweet, barely audible singing emerged from a thicket. I traced the song to a lobelia plant, commonly called "rabbit tobacco" or "life everlasting." Asthma had been troubling me, and so I gave this plant some of my hair in exchange for some of her leaves. From drinking a mild tea made from the leaves, my asthma cleared up. If my mind had not been still, I never would have heard this healing plant.

Through stillness, I find my center. I can be many things to many people, but in reality, I have to be true to myself and to my spiritual calling. This helps to create harmony, and when someone lives in harmony with their surroundings and themselves, they touch everything around them in a good way—loved ones, strangers, animals, the very earth herself. Their loving steps on the earth can be like the healing touch of an acupuncturist stimulating the body's meridians.

This realization hits home whenever I cross the routes that my fellow walkers and I have traversed throughout the United States. Even in a car with rubber, steel, and polyester insulating me from the ground, I feel something special—our collective love, hopes, dreams, and visions. The walks have, in a sense, become part of the earth's soul, something that lives on. That is what happens when people love and care enough and follow a vision.

On the walks, native elders often stressed that what we were doing was more important than we thought. This was a mystery to me at first, but, over time, I began to understand what they meant. When you connect with someone on a deep level, it can set off chain reactions that can affect relationships and decisions for years to come and with people you've never met. The full impact of the walks may never be known, but I like to think that new visions have emerged as a result.

Other walkers and I hold periodic reunions so that we can reconnect, touch the magic again, and leave inspired to action. Whether it is in teaching young people, becoming social and environmental activists or advocates, or simply being loving parents and human beings, walkers continue to touch those around them in positive ways. Now, some of our teenage children are considering their own walk. True visions live on. They grow and branch out like a great tree, and they produce offspring. They remind us of a larger plan and purpose set forth by the Creator.

Part of what I envisioned while gazing at the sun-dance pole many years ago was the overall regreening of the planet. It is what I glimpse in the wee hours at the annual Green Corn Ceremony. Hope. Healing. Renewal. The pulse of life growing stronger.

The doers, seekers, and visionaries have much more climbing to do if they—if we—are to establish a sane future. But isn't the knowledge that the path is ongoing part of the journey's magic?

Just at dawn in Hasbrook Park, I eventually ambled to the fenced holding pond and peered in, to a place where humans—and mowers—rarely ventured. Two female mallards squawked. A yellow-winged blackbird called from a limb. Fat robins flitted about.

Inside the fence, two blooming wildflowers, a white and a purple one, grew among the unkempt grass. They might have been prairie species, the last speck of wildness in my boyhood neighborhood. They seemed a thousand feet tall.

EPILOGUE

After I returned from Illinois to Florida, my job with *Florida Wildlife Magazine* ended, along with the magazine. It was, however, a death with dignity. We published an anthology celebrating fifty-six years of publication. Eventually, the magazine was revived, but with a focus on hunting and fishing.

Fortunately, I then landed a new job as a nature-based recreation writer and photographer for the state of Florida. By that fall, I was embarking on extended sea-kayaking trips along the expansive saltwater prairies of Florida's Big Bend Coast, helping to map a long-distance paddling trail.

In late summer 2005, my own agenda was dwarfed when Hurricane Katrina, the most devastating storm in recorded history, struck the Gulf Coast. Hundreds lost their lives; many thousands more lost their homes. Other violent storms followed, making 2005 the busiest hurricane season on record. In our area, Katrina was followed by the driest fall season in memory, while persistent rains flooded the northeastern states. Something was out of whack. Was this a wake-up call for us to look at how we were affecting the planet, especially in regard to global warming?

Surely, we can temper the impacts of current and future earth changes by creating more sustainable lifestyles. We can lessen our addictions to energy and material goods, embrace renewable resource options, and grow wholesome foods closer to home. Coupled with these lifestyle changes is a need to establish a sense of community in which people are mutually supported and spiritually linked.

Destructive hurricanes and other disasters often prompt me to reflect upon the Hopi prophecies. In 1948, traditional Hopi leaders met and selected four interpreters to share the time-honored prophecies of their people to the world. Thomas Banyacya of Kykotsmovi, whom we heard present Hopi prophecy on the Walk for the Earth (see chapter 11), was one of the four. He survived the longest, not passing away until 1999 at the age of eighty-nine.

The Hopi prophecy may vary from clan to clan and, in its entirety, can take several days to tell and several years to fully comprehend. What follows is only a brief summary:

Hopi teachings describe four cycles, or four worlds, of human life. During the first cycle, all humans spoke one language and lived in perfect balance. But they eventually misused their spiritual powers, leading to the world's downfall when the land sunk and earthquakes separated the land.

The second cycle evolved similarly to the first and was destroyed by the great Ice Age.

In the third cycle, the people also spoke one language. They developed a sophisticated technology and turned away from natural laws in a quest for material things. A great flood destroyed this world.

At the beginning of the fourth cycle, the Great Spirit gave people different languages and sent them to all four corners of the world, instructing them to care for the Earth and all life. But the Hopi predicted long ago that this world—the one we currently live in—would one day be rocked by powerful technologies. Their term for one such technology is a "gourd of ashes," which is believed to be the atomic bomb. They predicted three world wars. In 1992, Thomas Banyacya stated that the Persian Gulf War was the beginning of World War Three, but that spiritual forces had stopped it to allow humans to weigh their future choices.[1]

Hopi traditionalists believe that the Four Corners area, together with the four mountains that surround it, is sacred and will have a special purpose for the future of humankind—for those, that is, with peace in their hearts. This is one important reason that the area should be left in its natural state. If the power under the Four Corners is used for destruction, as, for instance, it would be if the uranium there were mined to make atomic bombs, a "Terrible Punishment" will follow.

According to Banyacya in 1992, warning signs of the impending great purification of this fourth cycle include an increase in floods, more damaging hurricanes, hailstorms, climate changes, earthquakes, and unusual behavior by animals. "It is up to all of us, as children of Mother Earth," he said, "to clean up this mess before it's too late."[2] He warned that the endless quest for material wealth would destroy the world's balance.

Central in the Hopi prophecy is a prediction that a white man would come to help transform the continent into a spiritual paradise. Called "Pahana" or the "True White Brother," this man would wear a red cap and cloak and bring sacred symbols and a fragment of stone that originally came from a Hopi holy stone thousands of years old. He would help the Indian people transform the continent with a spiritual revolution, leading people into greater attunement with the Great Spirit. Until his arrival, Hopi and other native people must keep their spiritual ways so they can show others how to live in harmony with each other and their surroundings.

It is not known whether the True White Brother is a single person or symbolically represents a group of people. Some Hopi believe Tibetan rinpoches and lamas signify the True White Brother, since they wear red and make sand paintings as a healing and meditation tool.

Many believe that seeds for the fifth cycle have already been planted in the hearts of humble people everywhere. These people will reestablish a world that is new and beautiful. Hopi elders speak about building a spiritual ark to help people emerge into this fifth cycle. During the earth changes, this fortress of peace will be stronger than that of any on the material plane.

The Hopi, along with traditional people worldwide, believe it is their role to uphold global balance through their ceremonies and lifestyles. As tribal life has eroded, the hefty burden has fallen on fewer and fewer people. It is now up to everyone, through prayers, thoughts, and actions, to share

the responsibility of keeping life in harmonious synchro-
nization. To create a peaceful and beautiful world for the
unborn is perhaps our highest purpose.

A great adventure lies ahead, one that will present us
with critical choices and challenges. I pray that we will
adhere to that old Quaker adage, slightly altered, to "live
simply so that others—and the earth's creatures—may
simply live."

NOTES

(For full citations, see bibliography)

CHAPTER 4
1. Lewis, Jr. and Jordan, *Creek Indian Medicine Ways*, 66.
2. Ibid., 67
3. James H. Howard, with Willie Lena, *Oklahoma Seminoles*, 211.
4. Perry, *Life with the Little People*, 40.
5. Eaton, *I Send a Voice*, 38.
6. Gardner, "Peyote Use," online article.

CHAPTER 6
1. DeLoria, *Custer Died for Your Sins*, 27.

CHAPTER 11
1. Waters, *Book of the Hopi*, 301–21.

CHAPTER 12
1. Black Elk, *The Sacred Pipe*, 127.
2. Ibid., 137.

CHAPTER 13
1. U.S. Department of Health and Human Services, "American Indians," online article.
2. Newhouse, "Bane of the Blackfeet," online article.
3. Ibid.

CHAPTER 14
1. Beech, "The Eagle and the Condor," online article.

CHAPTER 15
1. Bear Heart, with Larkin, *The Wind Is My Mother*, 6–7.
2. Ibid.

3. King, Martin Luther, Jr., *Autobiography*, 315.

CHAPTER 16
1. Toland, *Adolf Hitler*, 802.

CHAPTER 17
1. Teale, *Journey into Summer*, 75.

CHAPTER 18
1. Hudson, *The Southeastern Indians*, 365–75.
2. Black Hawk, *Autobiography*, 93–94.
3. Buffalo Bird Woman, *Buffalo Bird Woman's Garden*, 27.
4. Black Hawk, *Autobiography*, 93–94.
5. Ibid., 101.
6. Ibid., 102
7. Ibid.
8. Lincoln, *Collected Works*, vol 3, 511–12.

CHAPTER 19
1. Bryant, *Poetical Works*, 184–89.
2. Steele, *A Summer Journey*, online excerpt.
3. Short, "Observations," 117.
4. Leopold, *A Sand County Almanac*, 189.
5. McLean, *William Cullen Bryant*, 128.
6. Beloit Daily News, "Tribes Consider Casinos in Illinois," online article.
7. Kimberly, "Tribe Puts Money on Farmland," online article.
8. Illinois State Museum, online article.

CHAPTER 20
1. Ray, *Wild Card Quilt*, 9.

EPILOGUE
1. Banyacya, Address to the United Nations, online article.
2. Ibid.

BIBLIOGRAPHY

Abourezk, James G., "James G. Abourezk, Papers 1970-1983." L. D. Weeks Library, University of South Dakota, Vermillion, South Dakota, March 28, 2002. http://www.usd.edu/library/special/abourezkjg.htm.

Ali, Saleem H. *Mining, the Environment, and Indigenous Development Conflicts.* Tucson: University of Arizona Press, 2003.

Andrews, Kathy. "Saving Illinois' Treasures." *Outdoor Illinois,* September 2003, 11–13.

———. "Life on the Prairie." *Outdoor Illinois,* April 2003, 14–17.

Banyacya, Thomas. Address to the United Nations General Assembly. New York, December 10, 1992, The Alpha Institute, http://www.alphacdc.com/banyacya/un92.html.

Bear Heart, with Molly Larkin. *The Wind Is My Mother: The Life and Teachings of a Native American Shaman.* New York: Clarkson Potter, 1996.

Beech, Laverne. "The Eagle and the Condor Join Together in Ceremony." *Wellbriety!* White Bison's Online Magazine, Summer/Fall 2003. http://www.whitebison.org/magazine/2003/volume4/vol4no21.html.

Benedek, Emily. *The Wind Won't Know Me: A History of the Navajo-Hopi Land Dispute.* New York: Knopf, 1992.

"Bison Grazing Increases Biodiversity in Grasslands." National Science Foundation press release, April 30, 1998.

Black Elk. *Black Elk Speaks*. Recorded by John G. Neihardt. Lincoln and London: University of Nebraska Press, 1985.

Black Elk. *The Sacred Pipe: Black Elk's Account of the Seven Rites of the Oglala Sioux*. Recorded and edited by Joseph Eppes Brown. Norman and London: University of Oklahoma Press, 1989.

Black Hawk. *Autobiography of Ma-Ka-Tai-Me-She-Kia-Kaik, or Black Hawk*. Interpreted by Antoine LeClair. Edited by J. B. Patterson. St. Louis: Press of Continental Printing Company, 1882.

Blumberg, Alex. "Adventures in the Rhizosphere." *Chicago Wilderness*, Spring 1999, 10–14.

Bryant, William Cullen, *Poetical Works of William Cullen Bryant*. New York: D. Appleton & Co., 1854.

Buffalo Bird Woman (Maxi'diwiac). *Buffalo Bird Woman's Garden*. As told to Gilbert Livingstone Wilson. St. Paul: Minnesota Historical Society, 1987. (Originally *Agriculture of the Hidatsa Indians: An Indian Interpretation* by Gilbert Livingstone Wilson. PhD thesis. Minneapolis: University of Minnesota, 1917.)

DeLoria, Vine. *Custer Died for Your Sins*. New York: Macmillan, 1970.

Dietrich, Chris and David Voegtlin. "Prescribed Burning and Prairie Insects: Can We Have Both?" *The Illinois Steward,* Summer 2001, 11–13.

Eaton, Evelyn. *I Send a Voice*. Wheaton, IL: Theosophical Publishing House, Quest Books, 1978.

Ehle, John. *Trail of Tears: The Rise and Fall of the Cherokee Nation*, New York: Doubleday, 1988.

Encyclopedia of North American Indians. "American Indian Movement (AIM)." Houghton Mifflin Online Study Center, 2005. http://college.hmco.com/history/readerscomp/naind/html/na_001600_americanind2.htm.

Foreman, Grant. *The Five Civilized Tribes*. Norman: University of Oklahoma Press, 1986.

Friederici, Peter. "Where the Wild Ones Are." *Chicago Wilderness*, premiere issue 1997, 6–9.

Gardner, Amanda. "Peyote Use by Native Americans Doesn't Damage Brain." *HealthDay News*. Distributed by the New York Times Syndicate, November 4, 2005, online article, http://12.31.13.60/healthnews/healthday/051104HD528941.htm.

"Grand Prairie." Grand Prairie Friends, July 24, 2006. http://www.prairienet.org/gpf/grandprairie.php.

Guise, Paula. "Navaho-Hopi Long Land Dispute." Website article, 1996, 1997. http://www.kstrom.net/isk/maps/az/navhopi.html.

Henrichs, Lisa. "Grazing As a Technique for Prairie Restoration." http://horticulture.coafes.umn.edu/vd/h5015/97papers/henrichs.html.

Hoebel, E. Adamson. *The Cheyennes: Indians of the Great Plains*. New York: Holt, Rinehart and Winston, 1960.

Howard, James H., with Willie Lena. *Oklahoma Seminoles: Medicines, Magic, and Religion*. Norman and London: University of Oklahoma Press, 1990.

BIBLIOGRAPHY

Howard, Robert P. *Illinois: A History of the Prairie State.* Grand Rapids, MI: William B. Kerdmans Publishing Company, 1972.

Hudson, Charles. *The Southeastern Indians.* Knoxville: University of Tennessee Press, 1982.

Illinois Department of Natural Resources. *Goose Lake Prairie State Natural Area.* Brochure, 2001.

————. *Midewin National Tallgrass Prairie.* Brochure.

Illinois Department of Conservation. *Goose Lake Prairie Trail Guide.* Brochure.

Illinois State Museum. "Prairies in the Prairie State." Online article, 2003. http://www.museum.state.il.us/exhibits/midewin/index.html.

Jahoda, Gloria. *The Trail of Tears: The Story of American Indian Removals 1813–1855.* New York: Holt, Rinehart and Winston, 1975.

Johnson, Senator Tim (D-SD). Opening statement to Hearing on the Federal Reserve's First Monetary Policy Report to Congress for 2002. U. S. Senate Committee on Banking, Housing, and Urban Affairs, March 7, 2002.

Kimberly, James. "Tribe Puts Money on Farmland . . . Casino?" *Chicago Tribune*, May 9, 2006, online article, http://www.chicagotribune.com/.

King, Jr., Martin Luther. *Autobiography of Martin Luther King, Jr.* Edited by Clayborne Carson. New York: Warner Books, 1998.

Kansas State University. *Konza Prairie Biological Station.* Online publication, 2003. http://www.ksu.edu/konza.

Lewis, Jr., David and Ann T. Jordan. *Creek Indian Medicine Ways.* Albuquerque: University of New Mexico Press, 2002.

Laubin, Reginald and Gladys Laubin. *The Indian Tipi: Its History, Construction, and Use.* New York: Ballantine, 1977.

Leopold, Aldo. *A Sand County Almanac.* New York and Oxford: Oxford University Press, 1989.

Lincoln, Abraham. *Collected Works of Abraham Lincoln.* Edited by Roy P. Basler. New Brunswick, NJ: Rutgers University Press, 1953.

Lott, Dale F. *American Bison: A Natural History.* Berkeley and Los Angeles: University of California Press, 2002.

Mails, Thomas E. *The Hopi Survival Kit.* New York: Penguin Books, 1997.

Marriott, Alice and Carol K. Rachlin. *Peyote.* New York and Scarborough, Ontario: Mentor Books, 1972.

McLean, Albert F. Jr. *William Cullen Bryant.* New York: Twayne Publishers, 1964.

McIntyre, Mac. "Land of the Giant Trees." DeKalb County, Illinois. Online article, 1998. http://www.dekalbcounty-il.com/shabbona.html.

McQuilkin, Geoffrey, coexecutive director of Mono Lake Committee. Dinner address to Walker Lake Summit, April 2, 2002.

Meek, Miki. "Compensating Life Downwind of Nevada." *National Geographic Magazine Online Extra*, November, 2002. http://magma.nationalgeographic.com/ngm/0211/feature1/online_extra.html.

Miller, Timothy. "Native American Church." The Religious Movements Homepage Project of the University of Virginia, March 24, 2004. http://religiousmovements.lib.virginia.edu/nrms/nachurch.htm.

Mitchell, Gary. *Stories of the Potawatomi People.* Online version, 1997. http://www.kansasheritage.org/pbp/books/mitch/mitchbuk.html.

Nance, Dave. "The Story of Anderson Prairie Park—The Prairie Journal." Class curriculum essay, Pana High School, Pana, IL, 2005.

NativeTech: Native American Technology and Art. "Native American History of Corn." Online article, 2003. http://www.nativetech.org/cornhusk/cornhusk.html.

"Navajo Nation President Joe Shirley, Jr. Signs Dine Natural Resources Protection Act of 2005." Navajo Nation press release, April 30, 2005.

Newhouse, Eric. "Bane of the Blackfeet." *Great Falls Tribune,* August 22, 1999, online article, http://www.gannett.com/go/difference/greatfalls/pages/part8/blackfeet.html.

Nies, Judith. "The Black Mesa Syndrome: Indian Lands, Black Gold." Online article, 2005. http://www.shundahai.org/bigmtbackground.html.

Nieves, Evelyn. "On Pine Ridge, a String of Broken Promises." *The Washington Post,* October 21, 2004.

Northern Illinois University. "Chief Shabbona." Online article. http://www3.niu.edu/historicalbuildings/leaders_shabbona.htm.

Pana Natural Heritage Society. "Anderson Prairie." Online article, 2003. http://www.andersonprairie.org/.

Paredes, Anthony J. *Indians of the Southeastern United States in the Late 20th Century*. Tuscaloosa and London: University of Alabama Press, 1992.

Perry, Robert Johnson. *Life with the Little People*. Greenfield Center, NY: The Greenfield Review Press, 1998.

Ray, Janisse. *Wild Card Quilt*. Minneapolis: Milkweed Editions, 2003.

Riddell, Jill. "Midewin Prairie Rises from Vast Site of Joliet Arsenal, Nurturing a Healing Grassland." *Chicago Tribune*, August 9, 1996.

Sandburg, Carl. *Selected Poems*. New York and Avenel, NJ: Gramercy Books, 1992.

"Shabbona: Friend of the White Men." Forest Preserve District of Cook County. Nature Bulletin no. 748, March 21, 1964.

Short, C. W. "Observations on the Botany of Illinois, more especially with reference to the autumnal flora of the prairies." *Western Journal of Medicine and Surgery*, New Series 3, 1845.

Shundahai Network. Group website, December 2005. http://www.shundahai.org/Shundahai_Network_Information.htm.

Spivey-Weber, Frances, and Geoffrey McQuilkin and Lisa Cutting. "Mono Lake Policy Today." Mono Lake Newsletter, Summer 2003.

Steele, Eliza. *A Summer Journey in the West*. New York: Arno Press, 1975. (Reprint of 1841 edition by J. S. Taylor of New York.), online excerpt, Midewin Tallgrass Prairie website, http://www.openlands.org/midewin/steele.html.

Swanton, John R. *The Indians of the Southeastern United States.* Washington and London: Smithsonian Institution Press, 1979.

———. *Myths and Tales of the Southeastern Indians.* Norman and London: University of Oklahoma Press, 1995.

Teale, Edwin Way. *Journey into Summer.* New York: Dodd, Mead, 1960.

"The Story of John Deere." John Deere Company, 2003. http://www.deere.com/en_US/compinfo/history/.

Toland, John. *Adolf Hitler.* Garden City, NY: Doubleday, 1976.

"Tribes Consider Casinos in Illinois." *Beloit Daily News*, September 18, 1998, online article, http://www.beloitdailynews.com/.

United States Department of Agriculture. *Midewin National Tallgrass Prairie Fact Sheet.* January 2003.

United States Department of Health and Human Services. "American Indians/Alaska Natives and Substance Abuse." Prevention Alert 5, no. 16 (November 22, 2002), online article, http://www.ncadi.samhsa.gov/.

"Uranium Impact Assessment." Southwest Research and Information Center Uranium Impact Assessment Program Website, December 2005. http://www.sric.org/uranium/index.html.

Waters, Frank. *Book of the Hopi.* New York: Penguin Books, 1986.

Watson, Danny. "Henslow's Sparrow." *Kentucky Afield*, Summer 2003, 20–21.

White, John. "How the Terms Savanna, Barrens, and Oak Openings Were Used in Early Illinois," United States Environmental Protection Agency, 1991, http://www.epa.gov/greatlakes/ecopage/upland/oak/oak94/Proceedings/White.html.

"Winnebago Indian Reservation." Tribal website, 2005. http://www.winnebagotribe.com/aboutus.htm.

Yellowman, Gordon. "Cheyenne and Arapaho History." Tribal website, 2005. http://www.cheyenneandarapaho.org/.

INDEX

INDEX

INDEX

INDEX

INDEX

QUEST BOOKS

encourages open-minded inquiry into
world religions, philosophy, science, and the arts
in order to understand the wisdom of the ages,
respect the unity of all life, and help people explore
individual spiritual self-transformation.

Its publications are generously supported by
The Kern Foundation,
a trust committed to Theosophical education.

Quest Books is the imprint of
the Theosophical Publishing House,
a division of the Theosophical Society in America.
For information about programs, literature,
on-line study, membership benefits, and international centers,
see www.theosophical.org
or call 800-669-1571 or (outside the U.S.) 630-668-1571.

Related Quest Titles

*Manual for the Peacemaker: An Iroquois Legend
to Heal Self and Society*, by Jean Houston, with
Margaret Rubin

Native Healer, by Medicine Grizzlybear Lake

The Shaman and the Medicine Wheel, by Evelyn Eaton

Shamanism, edited by Shirley J. Nicholson

To order books or a complete Quest catalog,
call 800-669-9425 or (outside the U.S.) 630-665-0130.

*Praise for **Doug Alderson's***
THE VISION KEEPERS

"We will all benefit as Doug Alderson shows us the sacred path of the elders. He has learned to use that knowledge, which we call Wisdom, and share it with the rest of the world so that we may all meet the Great Spirit through the ancient spiritual practice of walking."
—MARCELLUS BEAR HEART WILLIAMS, Muskogee Nation, Creek Tribe; author of *The Wind Is My Mother*

"Doug Alderson's initiation into Native American spirituality and environmental affairs combined with his experiences while completing the arduous walks makes a profound statement: Visions can become a reality, which in turn serve to give us purpose and meaning."
—MEDICINE GRIZZLYBEAR LAKE, traditional healer; author of *Native Healer: Initiation into an Ancient Art*

"Alderson recaptures the rewards of physical and spiritual travel similar to those of medieval pilgrims as they walked great distances. . . . I can give no greater praise than to say this is the one book that never leaves my bedside table!"
—DR. KENT REILLY III, director, Center for the Study of Arts and Symbolism of Ancient America, University of Texas

"Doug is a good-hearted man of traditional knowledge, integrity, and substance, and he is a trusted colleague within the realm of traditional Muscogee ceremonialism. It pleases me to know that his story is being shared with the general public."
—DANIEL PENTON, senior archaeologist; traditional chief of the Muscogee Nation of Florida

"We can be grateful for the unabashed, yet humble spirituality Alderson has learned to fuse with his activism, and for his willingness to share with us his enormous heart."
—SUSAN CERULEAN, author of *Tracking Desire: A Journey after Swallow-tailed Kites*